VOLUME 3
NEW TESTAMENT

THE NEW COLLEGEVILLE
BIBLE COMMENTARY

THE GOSPEL ACCORDING TO

LUKE

Michael F. Patella, O.S.B.

SERIES EDITOR

Daniel Durken, O.S.B.

LITURGICAL PRESS

Collegeville, Minnesota

www.litpress.org

Nihil obstat: Robert C. Harren, *Censor deputatus.*
Imprimatur: ✠ John F. Kinney, Bishop of St. Cloud, Minnesota, August 30, 2005.

Design by Ann Blattner.

4	5	6	7	8	9

Library of Congress Cataloging-in-Publication Data

Patella, Michael, 1954–
  The Gospel according to Luke / Michael F. Patella.
    p. cm. — (The new Collegeville Bible commentary. New Testament ; v. 3)
    Summary: "Complete biblical texts with sound, scholarly based commentary that is written at a pastoral level; the Scripture translation is that of the New American Bible with Revised New Testament and Revised Psalms (1991)" —Provided by publisher.
    ISBN-13: 978-0-8146-2862-1 (pbk. : alk. paper)
    ISBN-10: 0-8146-2862-1 (pbk. : alk. paper)
    1. Bible. N.T. Luke--Commentaries.   I. Title.   II. Series.

BS259 25.53.P44   2005
226.4'077—dc22

2005008467

CONTENTS

Abbreviations   4

THE GOSPEL ACCORDING TO LUKE

Introduction   5

Text and Commentary   9

  The Prologue (1:1-4)   9

  The Infancy Narrative (1:5–2:52)   10

  Preparation for the Public Ministry (3:1–4:13)   23

  The Ministry in Galilee (4:14–9:50)   29

  The Journey to Jerusalem (9:51–19:27)   69

  Teaching Ministry in Jerusalem (19:28–21:38)   125

  The Passion (22:1–23:56)   139

  The Resurrection (24:1-53)   153

Review Aids and Discussion Topics   159

Index of Citations from the
  Catechism of the Catholic Church   163

Maps   167

Books of the Bible

Acts—Acts of the Apostles
Amos—Amos
Bar—Baruch
1 Chr—1 Chronicles
2 Chr—2 Chronicles
Col—Colossians
1 Cor—1 Corinthians
2 Cor—2 Corinthians
Dan—Daniel
Deut—Deuteronomy
Eccl (or Qoh)—Ecclesiastes
Eph—Ephesians
Esth—Esther
Exod—Exodus
Ezek—Ezekiel
Ezra—Ezra
Gal—Galatians
Gen—Genesis
Hab—Habakkuk
Hag—Haggai
Heb—Hebrews
Hos—Hosea
Isa—Isaiah
Jas—James
Jdt—Judith
Jer—Jeremiah
Job—Job
Joel—Joel
John—John
1 John—1 John
2 John—2 John
3 John—3 John
Jonah—Jonah
Josh—Joshua
Jude—Jude
Judg—Judges
1 Kgs—1 Kings

2 Kgs—2 Kings
Lam—Lamentations
Lev—Leviticus
Luke—Luke
1 Macc—1 Maccabees
2 Macc—2 Maccabees
Mal—Malachi
Mark—Mark
Matt—Matthew
Mic—Micah
Nah—Nahum
Neh—Nehemiah
Num—Numbers
Obad—Obadiah
1 Pet—1 Peter
2 Pet—2 Peter
Phil—Philippians
Phlm—Philemon
Prov—Proverbs
Ps(s)—Psalms
Rev—Revelation
Rom—Romans
Ruth—Ruth
1 Sam—1 Samuel
2 Sam—2 Samuel
Sir—Sirach
Song—Song of Songs
1 Thess—1 Thessalonians
2 Thess—2 Thessalonians
1 Tim—1 Timothy
2 Tim—2 Timothy
Titus—Titus
Tob—Tobit
Wis—Wisdom
Zech—Zechariah
Zeph—Zephaniah

Other Ancient Sources

Ant.   Josephus, *Jewish Antiquities*
Aug.   Suetonius, *Divus Augustus*
J.W.   Josephus, *Jewish War*

The Gospel According to Luke

The Gospel of Luke, the third Gospel in the New Testament canon, has a remarkable place in the study of Sacred Scripture, and this unique position does not stem solely from the fact that it is the only Gospel to have a second volume associated with it, namely, the Acts of the Apostles. Luke engenders a great deal of discussion on the level of New Testament formation, sensitivity to historical data, literary technique, and theological development. This commentary deals with these areas to a greater or lesser degree.

The Gospel message

Each Gospel relates a particular evangelist's theological interpretation of the kerygma, that is, the passion, death, and resurrection of Jesus. To do this, the Gospel writer takes events from Jesus' life as passed down from traditions and sources and composes a Gospel account. Under the inspiration of the Holy Spirit, an evangelist uses his composition to present his particular theology of redemption mediated through Christ's life. Details may or may not be accurate, but the truth of the Gospel goes beyond details. The central focus of this study, therefore, is the theological picture that Luke's Gospel paints of Jesus, his earthly ministry, and the early church.

Matthew, Mark, Luke, and John

Anyone reading the Gospels notices that there are stories within them that overlap, parallel, and seemingly copy each other. The reason for, and explanation of, this problem have been part of the church since the beginning. Scholars such as Origen and Augustine were among the first to develop theories on the formation of the Gospels. In the modern era, new theories have arisen that have continued the dialogue and discussion on the development of the New Testament.

The brevity of this commentary prevents any lengthy discussion of the sources Luke used in writing his Gospel; this question has an involved and complicated history. For simplicity's sake, our commentary notes the names of commonly held sources as well as the familiar vocabulary of biblical scholarship. Knowing the following terms will be most helpful:

- *Canon:* the official collection of books comprising the Bible.
- *Codex Sinaiticus* and *Codex Vaticanus:* two of the most dependable, extant New Testament manuscripts.
- Eschaton: the final times bringing God's eternal plan to fulfillment. The study and interpretation of the eschaton is called eschatology.
- *Evangelist:* the name given to the four Gospel writers: Matthew, Mark, Luke, and John.
- *Kerygma:* the proclamation of the passion, death, and resurrection of Christ that also describes how salvation comes through participation in the same passion, death, and resurrection.
- *Parallel:* a term used to describe a passage in one Gospel that has a like passage in another Gospel.
- *Q:* a hypothetical, oral source that contains material common to Matthew and Luke but not Mark.
- *Synoptics:* the Gospels of Matthew, Mark, and Luke, so named because they share so much of the same narrative line as well as the same material.
- *Textual witness:* early written documents containing all or part of the biblical canon.

Luke the evangelist

Not much is known about the evangelist Luke. The tradition says that he was both a physician and an artist from Syria who completed his Gospel between A.D. 80 and 90. Using Acts 20–28 as a guide, along with Colossians 4:14 and Philemon 1:24, many feel that he may have known Paul. Although it is impossible to prove these claims, the texts that Luke wrote indicate that he was a highly educated person, influential in the early church, aware of geography (outside Palestine anyway) and history, and very much attuned to the dynamic, direction, and development of Christianity.

Sensitivity to historical data

In addition to being considered a doctor and an artist, many have thought of Luke as a historian, because he gives greater attention to historical details than any other evangelist. For example, passages describing the birth of Jesus and the ministry of John the Baptist contain information on emperors, governors, and kings, and a good deal of it is close to accurate. Much of our information about Pontius Pilate comes from Luke. In large part, his information about the Herodian dynasty matches well with the writings of the ancient Jewish historian Flavius Josephus.

Literary technique

Luke is an economical writer. This evangelist avoids repetitions and superfluous information. He tells a story well, with attention given to rising action, climax, and denouement. His use of Greek is among the finest in the New Testament, and he is well-versed in Greco-Roman literary style. His prose has a nobility that has made this Gospel a favorite of many.

Theological development

Luke views the passion, death, and resurrection of Christ as the great salvific act that has affected the whole cosmos. The evangelist expresses this theology by presenting Jesus' earthly ministry as a battle between Christ and Satan. Christ's victory over evil comes with his death and resurrection. In Lukan theology, the death on the cross is actually a transfiguration into glory. Furthermore, by virtue of that death, the same transformative glory is promised to humanity, a concept that came to be known as *theosis*.

In this presentation, Luke relies on literary motifs to relay these key concepts. First, there is the motif of the diabolical force. Every good story needs an antagonist, and Luke elevates Satan to this position. Consequently, Christ's miracles and cures are more than kind deeds; they are attacks against the Evil One and his diabolical force. In other words, Christ is in a relentless pursuit of redeeming the world from Satan's clutches.

Second is the idea of the great reversal, a term used to describe the turn in fortune that will befall all between now and the *eschaton,* that is, the end times: the hungry now will have a banquet, while the rich go hungry; the humble will be exalted, and the exalted will be humbled.

Next, there is the schism motif. Christ will come to all, but some will heed his call to discipleship while others will not.

Finally, there is joy. The word appears more times in the Third Gospel than in any other New Testament work. In Lukan theology, for a world redeemed and transfigured by the blood of Christ, there can be no other Christian response than joy.

The Gospel According To Luke

I. The Prologue

1 ¹Since many have undertaken to compile a narrative of the events that have been fulfilled among us, ²just as those who were eyewitnesses from

THE PROLOGUE

Luke 1:1-4

1:1-4 Address to Theophilus

The Gospel opens with a short prologue of a single periodic sentence, a style typical of ancient literature that often sets the tone and purpose of biographies and histories. Josephus and Polybius, for example, show similar introductions. Luke's use of this style often raises the question of whether he sees himself as writing a biography or a history. Opinions favoring one or the other abound. Perhaps the most we can say is that Luke is simply following the literary convention of the day as he writes his two-volume work. The Gospel, neither a biography nor a history, is an evangelical proclamation. A Gentile audience would expect such a prologue, and Luke is simply supplying it.

The identity of Theophilus is unknown. Possibilities range from his being a benefactor of the community, a church leader, or even a civil authority. Perhaps Theophilus is all three. On the other hand, using the name Theophilus (literally, "Beloved of God") universalizes the identity and allows every reader to be the addressee.

The prologue provides hints at the formation of the New Testament as well as the development of the early Christian community. What are the "events that have been fulfilled"? Who are the "eyewitnesses" and "ministers of the word"? Luke describes some of these events and personages within his two-volume work, particularly in the Acts of the Apostles, but how much of it is recoverable is difficult to answer. Of fascinating interest

the beginning and ministers of the word have handed them down to us, [3]I too have decided, after investigating everything accurately anew, to write it down in an orderly sequence for you, most excellent Theophilus, [4]so that you may realize the certainty of the teachings you have received.

II. The Infancy Narrative

Announcement of the Birth of John. [5]In the days of Herod, King of Judea, there was a priest named Zechariah of the priestly division of Abijah; his wife was from the daughters of Aaron, and her name was Elizabeth. [6]Both were righteous in the eyes of God, observing all the commandments and ordinances of the Lord blamelessly. [7]But they had no child, because Elizabeth was barren and both were advanced in years. [8]Once when he was serving as priest in his division's turn before God, [9]according to the practice of the priestly service, he was chosen by lot to enter the sanctuary of the Lord to burn incense. [10]Then, when the whole assembly of the people

---

for source critics is Luke's explanation that he has investigated "everything accurately anew, to write it down in an orderly sequence." How many and varied were the initial documents before they saw their final editing at Luke's hand? Extant papyri, lectionaries, and targums certainly bespeak a Christian movement very much in ferment and development. Luke's project replaced the diverse gospel fragments floating around the Greco-Roman world. That this Gospel eventually became part of the New Testament canon attests to its nearly universal use over the course of the first two centuries.

THE INFANCY NARRATIVE

Luke 1:5–2:52

Only Matthew and Luke feature stories of the birth of Christ, although from two different perspectives. Luke centers his account on Mary, while Matthew focuses on Joseph. It is obvious that Matthew and Luke were not copying each other in forming their respective infancy narratives. Nonetheless, they do share some details. Both have an angel relaying the divine plan to the human participants—Joseph in Matthew, Mary in Luke. Both state that this child will be born of the house of David in Bethlehem, that his name will be Jesus, and that these events will occur while Herod the Great is king of Judea (37 B.C.–4 B.C.). Most importantly, despite the many variations in the two different accounts, the two agree on the essential point that Mary is pregnant, and there is no human father.

10

was praying outside at the hour of the incense offering, [11]the angel of the Lord appeared to him, standing at the right of the altar of incense. [12]Zechariah was troubled by what he saw, and fear came upon him. [13]But the angel said to him, "Do not be afraid, Zechariah, because your prayer has been heard. Your wife Elizabeth will bear you a son, and you shall name him John. [14]And you will have joy and gladness, and many will rejoice at his birth, [15]for he will be great in the sight of [the] Lord. He will drink neither wine nor strong drink. He will be filled with the holy Spirit even from his mother's womb, [16]and he will turn many of the children of Israel to the Lord their God. [17]He will go before him in the spirit and power of Elijah to turn the hearts of fathers toward children and the disobedient to the understanding of the righteous, to prepare a people fit for the Lord." [18]Then Zechariah said to the angel, "How shall I know this? For I am an old man, and my wife is advanced in years." [19]And the angel said

Luke's purpose for including the infancy narratives is to situate the whole Gospel within the story of God's divine plan. Luke also uses references and allusions to the Old Testament, especially prophetic figures. Furthermore, he has passages dealing with John the Baptist precede those of Jesus. This structure prepares the reader for an account that aims to show Jesus as the one long-promised to deliver humankind from sin and death. Luke's infancy narratives grab the attention of his Gentile audience, catechize them, and graft them to the community of Israel by setting the many references to political events and leaders of the day within the context of the Old Testament. As Simeon proclaims in his canticle (2:29-32), Jesus is "a light for revelation to the Gentiles, / and glory for [the] people Israel" (2:32). Furthermore, this glory will not come easily, for even Jesus' mother, Mary, will be pierced by a sword. Thus, the infancy narratives serve as an abbreviated version of the Gospel and Acts. In the Acts of the Apostles, Luke recounts how Peter, Paul, and the Gentiles receive the light of revelation, but only after hardship and pain. On the final page of Acts, Paul is living, preaching, and teaching in that most Gentile of cities, Rome.

1:5-25 Announcement of the birth of John the Baptist
Luke provides a broad context for Jesus' birth, employing both Old Testament prophecies and typologies. Zechariah and Elizabeth are described as being "advanced in years," and thus past the age of childbearing.

▶ This symbol indicates a cross reference number in the *Catechism of the Catholic Church*. See page 163 for number citations.

to him in reply, "I am Gabriel, who stand before God. I was sent to speak to you and to announce to you this good news. ²⁰But now you will be speechless and unable to talk until the day these things take place, because you did not believe my words, which will be fulfilled at their proper time."

²¹Meanwhile the people were waiting for Zechariah and were amazed that he stayed so long in the sanctuary. ²²But when he came out, he was unable to speak to them, and they realized that he had seen a vision in the sanctuary. He was gesturing to them but remained mute. ²³Then, when his days of ministry were completed, he went home. ²⁴After this time his wife Elizabeth conceived, and she went into seclusion for five months, saying, ²⁵"So has the Lord done for me at a time when he has seen fit to take away my disgrace before others."

Announcement of the Birth of Jesus. ²⁶In the sixth month, the angel Gabriel was sent from God to a town of Galilee called Nazareth, ²⁷to a virgin betrothed to a man named Joseph, of the house of David, and the virgin's name was Mary. ²⁸And coming to her, he said, "Hail, favored one! The Lord is with you." ²⁹But she was greatly troubled at what was said and pondered what sort of greeting this might be. ³⁰Then the angel said to her, "Do not be afraid, Mary, for you have found favor with God. ³¹Behold, you will conceive in your womb and bear a son, and you shall name him Jesus. ³²He will be great and will be called Son of the Most High, and the Lord God will give him the throne of David

---

The announcement of the Baptist's birth, therefore, is similar to the miraculous birth genre found with Abraham and Sarah (Gen 18:1-15), Manoah and his wife (Judg 13:2-25), and Elkanah and Hannah (1 Sam 1:1-23). In addition, both Zechariah and Elizabeth are of priestly stock, which means that their son John would one day be serving in the temple at Jerusalem. None of the evangelists, however, imply that John the Baptist ever took on this role.

As a priest, Zechariah would take his turn serving in the temple twice a year for a week at a time. This detail no doubt led to the tradition, dating from at least the sixth century, that Ein Karem, with its close proximity to Jerusalem, is the village of John's birth.

Angels are God's messengers and agents, and Luke mentions them twenty-five times in the Gospel. More than half of these occurrences fall within the first two chapters. The presence of an angel at the altar of incense (v. 11) underscores God's role in the events to follow. While in Matthew's Gospel the angel who appears to Joseph (1:20) remains unnamed, Luke specifies the identity of the heavenly messenger who comes to both Zechariah and Mary. The name Gabriel itself is a combination of two He-

his father, [33]and he will rule over the house of Jacob forever, and of his kingdom there will be no end." [34]But Mary said to the angel, "How can this be, since I have no relations with a man?" [35]And the angel said to her in reply, "The holy Spirit will come upon you, and the power of the Most High will overshadow you. Therefore the child to be born will be called holy, the Son of God. [36]And behold, Elizabeth, your relative, has also conceived a son in her old age, and this is the sixth month for her who was called barren; [37]for nothing will be impossible for God." [38]Mary said, "Behold, I am the handmaid of the Lord. May it be done to me according to your word." Then the angel departed from her.

Mary Visits Elizabeth. [39]During those days Mary set out and traveled to the hill country in haste to a town of Judah, [40]where she entered the house of Zechariah and greeted Elizabeth. [41]When Elizabeth heard Mary's greeting, the infant leaped in her womb, and Elizabeth, filled with the holy Spirit, [42]cried out in a loud voice and said, "Most blessed are you among women, and blessed is the fruit of your womb. [43]And how does this happen to me, that the mother of my Lord should come to me? [44]For at the moment the sound of your greeting reached my ears, the infant in my womb leaped for joy. [45]Blessed are you who believed that what was spoken to you by the Lord would be fulfilled."

---

brew terms, *Gabur* ("strong man," "warrior"), and *El* ("God"), therefore "Warrior of God." Gabriel has a role in the Old Testament. In the book of Daniel, this angel explains a vision to Daniel (8:17-26) while simultaneously giving Daniel understanding (9:22).

1:26-45 Announcement of the birth of Jesus and Mary's pregnancy

In Luke's chronology, Gabriel's announcement to Zechariah (1:8-20) precedes the one to Mary (1:26-38). Luke is setting the proper sequence of salvation history. If John is the precursor of Jesus in the ministry, he must also come first in the order of birth. In the sixth month of Elizabeth's pregnancy, Gabriel comes to Nazareth to deliver the news to Mary. Of course, Mary is extremely puzzled by this information, and when she expresses her doubt (v. 29), Gabriel encourages her. When Zechariah doubts, however, he is made mute (vv. 18, 20).

Whatever point Luke is trying to make by this comparison of the two personages, it is not too clear. Perhaps it is another way to indicate the Baptist's subservience to Christ, a point reiterated by the baby's leaping in Elizabeth's womb upon hearing Mary's greeting. Or since the recovery of Zechariah's voice excites wonder in the people (vv. 60-64), Zechariah's muteness reflects Luke's attention to the details of storytelling; it advances the theme and the plot.

The Canticle of Mary. [46]And Mary said:

"My soul proclaims the greatness of the Lord;
[47]my spirit rejoices in God my savior.
[48]For he has looked upon his handmaid's lowliness;
behold, from now on will all ages call me blessed.
[49]The Mighty One has done great things for me,
and holy is his name.
[50]His mercy is from age to age to those who fear him.
[51]He has shown might with his arm, dispersed the arrogant of mind and heart.
[52]He has thrown down the rulers from their thrones
but lifted up the lowly.
[53]The hungry he has filled with good things;
the rich he has sent away empty.
[54]He has helped Israel his servant, remembering his mercy,
[55]according to his promise to our fathers,
to Abraham and to his descendants forever."

[56]Mary remained with her about three months and then returned to her home.

The Birth of John. [57]When the time arrived for Elizabeth to have her child she gave birth to a son. [58]Her neighbors and relatives heard that the Lord had shown his great mercy toward her, and they rejoiced with her. [59]When they came on the eighth day to circumcise the child, they were going to call him Zechariah after his father, [60]but his mother said in reply, "No. He will be called John." [61]But they answered her, "There is no one among your relatives who has this name." [62]So they made signs, asking his father what he wished him to be called. [63]He asked for a tablet and wrote, "John is his name," and all were amazed. [64]Immediately his mouth was opened, his tongue freed, and he spoke blessing God. [65]Then fear came upon all their neighbors, and all these matters were discussed throughout the

1:46-55 The Canticle of Mary

Traditionally called the *Magnificat* in the Western church where it is sung at Evening Prayer, the canticle has all the markings of an early hymn. There are four hymns in these opening narratives, of which this is the first. Grounded in a reference to Abraham and referencing other forebears, this song has a decidedly Jewish-Christian cast. The piece contains the reversal theme found in 1 Samuel 2:1-10, but it is modified. Those who oppress now will be overthrown, and the lowly will be exalted; those who are hungry now will have their fill, but those who are satiated now will be sent away.

1:57-80 The birth of John and the Canticle of Zechariah

Zechariah regains his speech upon acknowledging the divinely given name of his son. The hymn Zechariah sings, also known by its Latin

hill country of Judea. ⁶⁶All who heard these things took them to heart, saying, "What, then, will this child be?" For surely the hand of the Lord was with him.

The Canticle of Zechariah. ⁶⁷Then Zechariah his father, filled with the holy Spirit, prophesied, saying:

⁶⁸"Blessed be the Lord, the God of Israel,
for he has visited and brought
redemption to his people.
⁶⁹He has raised up a horn for our
salvation
within the house of David his
servant,
⁷⁰even as he promised through the
mouth of his holy
prophets from of old:
⁷¹salvation from our enemies
and from the hand
of all who hate us,
⁷²to show mercy to our fathers
and to be mindful of his holy
covenant
⁷³and of the oath he swore to
Abraham our father,
and to grant us that,

⁷⁴rescued from the hand of
enemies,
without fear we might worship him
⁷⁵in holiness and righteousness
before him all our days.
⁷⁶And you, child, will be called
prophet of the Most High,
for you will go before the Lord
to prepare his ways,
⁷⁷to give his people knowledge of
salvation
through the forgiveness of their
sins,
⁷⁸because of the tender mercy of our
God
by which the daybreak from on
high will visit us
⁷⁹to shine on those who sit in darkness and death's shadow,
to guide our feet into the path of
peace."

⁸⁰The child grew and became strong in spirit, and he was in the desert until the day of his manifestation to Israel.

The Birth of Jesus. ¹In those days a decree went out from Caesar Augustus that the whole world should be enrolled. ²This was the first enrollment,

---

name, the *Benedictus*, the Morning Prayer canticle in the Roman Office, clarifies John the Baptist's role in the sweep of salvation history. He is to "go before the Lord to prepare his ways" (v. 76). The beautiful, poetic images "daybreak from on high will visit us" (v. 78) and "to shine on those who sit in darkness and death's shadow" (v. 79) have their foundation in Isaiah 8:23–9:2. Luke concludes this section on John the Baptist with a brief note placing John in the desert, where the reader will encounter him again at the beginning of chapter 3. The evangelist now moves on to the birth of Christ.

2:1-7 The birth of Jesus

Scholars have often considered Luke's attention to historical detail as one indication of the evangelist's high level of education—not only for the

when Quirinius was governor of Syria. ³So all went to be enrolled, each to his own town. ⁴And Joseph too went up from Galilee from the town of Nazareth to Judea, to the city of David that is called Bethlehem, because he was of the house and family of David, ⁵to be enrolled with Mary, his betrothed, who was with child. ⁶While they were there, the time came for her to have her child, ⁷and she gave birth to her firstborn son. She wrapped him in swaddling clothes and laid him in a manger, because there was no room for them in the inn.

⁸Now there were shepherds in that region living in the fields and keeping the night watch over their flock. ⁹The angel of the Lord appeared to them and

fact that he includes such information but more for the way in which he uses it. Greco-Roman historians wrote their accounts to favor their patrons or the party in power, much the same way as a local chamber of commerce writes about its particular locale today. Thucydides, Tacitus, and Josephus all had a certain editorial slant to their works that supported those who supported them. Luke stands within this tradition, but with an important difference: his bias is toward showing the hand of the holy Spirit at work in both Jewish and Gentile events of the day. Jesus Christ is to be considered the fulfillment of both cultural worlds. We have observed an example of Jewish fulfillment in the stories of Zechariah, Elizabeth, and Mary. In these opening verses of chapter 2, we see the events in the pagan world also cooperating and foretelling the birth of the Messiah in Jesus Christ.

A difficulty enters into this section with the names and dates of the people mentioned. Although the Roman historian Suetonius states that there were registrations of Roman citizens in 28 B.C., 8 B.C., and A.D. 14 (*Divus Augustus* 27.5), there is no record, outside the New Testament, which states that Caesar Augustus (27 B.C.–A.D.14) decreed the enrollment of the whole empire, that is, non-citizens, for taxation or any other purposes. There were local registrations within various provinces from time to time, and once such census occurred under the Roman legate Quirinius, but he was not made governor of Syria until A.D. 6, when he also took control of Judea at the banishment of Herod's son Archelaus. Since Luke attests that both John the Baptist and Jesus were born under Herod the Great (37 B.C.–4 B.C.), most scholars concur that it would be impossible for these events to have occurred at a time when Caesar Augustus, Herod the Great, and Quirinius were all simultaneously in power.

For Luke's theological intention, however, the important point is that during the *Pax Romana*, when the Gentile world looked to Augustus Cae-

the glory of the Lord shone around them, and they were struck with great fear. [10]The angel said to them, "Do not be afraid; for behold, I proclaim to you good news of great joy that will be for all the people. [11]For today in the city of David a savior has been born for you who is Messiah and Lord. [12]And this will be a sign for you: you will find an infant wrapped in swaddling clothes and lying in a manger." [13]And suddenly there was a multitude of the heavenly host with the angel, praising God and saying:

> [14]"Glory to God in the highest
>   and on earth peace to those on
>   whom his favor rests."

sar as the prince of peace, Jesus comes into the world as the true Prince of Peace. In fulfillment of the Old Testament prophecies, which establish the messianic line through the house of David, Jesus, a descendant of David, is born in Bethlehem, the city of David. In order to make this point, Luke takes historical facts, such as the census, and reworks them to fit his theological purpose, just as ancient historians altered details to suit the purposes of their patrons. For contemporary readers, such remolding of details may seem spurious or dishonest, but in the religious tradition, the truth that Jesus is the Savior of the world lies beyond the accuracy of some facts dealing with the reigns of various rulers.

The Greek term *phatnē* is translated as "manger" (v. 7) but can also mean "stable." The Greek *kataluma*, represented here as "inn," specifically means "lodging" or "guestroom," with space for a dining area (*kataluma* is the word employed in Luke 22:11). Reading together both *phatnē* and *kataluma*, we can see that Luke is probably describing the typical house of the day. These homes, built for extended families, had a living space on the upper floors with a stable at ground level. Both Matthew and Luke emphasize Jesus' Davidic lineage through his foster father, Joseph, as well as the fact that Jesus is born in Bethlehem, the city of David. It is reasonable to conclude that Joseph had family in Bethlehem and that he and Mary stayed with them. With all the relatives of the extended family eating and sleeping in the upper *kataluma*, the one private place for Mary to give birth would be in the *phatnē* or stable.

According to Roman, Greek, Coptic, Armenian, and other ancient traditions, the phrase "firstborn son" (v. 7) represents a title of honor. It does not imply that Mary had other children after Jesus.

2:8-20 Angels and shepherds

Once again Luke uses an angel to announce a birth, this time to the shepherds. Shepherds, although not social outcasts, were among the

The Visit of the Shepherds. ¹⁵When the angels went away from them to heaven, the shepherds said to one another, "Let us go, then, to Bethlehem to see this thing that has taken place, which the Lord has made known to us." ¹⁶So they went in haste and found Mary and Joseph, and the infant lying in the manger. ¹⁷When they saw this, they made known the message that had been told them about this child. ¹⁸All who heard it were amazed by what had been told them by the shepherds. ¹⁹And Mary kept all these things, reflecting on them in her heart.

²⁰Then the shepherds returned, glorifying and praising God for all they had heard and seen, just as it had been told to them.

The Circumcision and Naming of Jesus. ²¹When eight days were completed for his circumcision, he was named Jesus, the name given him by the angel before he was conceived in the womb.

The Presentation in the Temple. ²²When the days were completed for their purification according to the law of Moses, they took him up to Jerusalem to present him to the Lord, ²³just as

poorest people in the society. A group composed mostly of women and young children, they did not own land or sheep, and they worked for hire. Luke underscores Jesus' salvific role especially for the poor with this annunciation story; the shepherds are the first to hear the good news. With the angelic choir (v. 14) we have the third song in the infancy narratives, the *Gloria*. In Western liturgies this text serves as the foundation for the "Glory to God."

2:21-38 Circumcision, naming, and presentation in the temple

The parallel between John the Baptist and Jesus continues in verse 21. John is circumcised and named eight days after his birth (1:59-60), and now so too with Jesus.

In portraying this section, Luke relies on some elements of the Mosaic Law as well as stories about the prophet Samuel (1 Sam 1:24-28). God commands Abraham to circumcise male descendants and slaves as a sign of the covenant (Gen 17:12), a point the book of Leviticus stipulates (12:3). Although Luke states that both parents must undergo the rites of purification (v. 22), the Levitical prescriptions apply only to the mother (Lev 12:2-5). A Gentile Christian himself, Luke is not always accurate in his explanation of Jewish cultic and legal codes. Luke rightly notes that the firstborn must be consecrated to the Lord (Exod 13:2), but this redemption is accomplished by paying five shekels to a priest (Num 3:47-48). The sacrifice of turtledoves Luke describes is part of a woman's purification rite. These verses serve to emphasize Mary and Joseph as

it is written in the law of the Lord, "Every male that opens the womb shall be consecrated to the Lord," ²⁴and to offer the sacrifice of "a pair of turtle-doves or two young pigeons," in accordance with the dictate in the law of the Lord.

²⁵Now there was a man in Jerusalem whose name was Simeon. This man was righteous and devout, awaiting the consolation of Israel, and the holy Spirit was upon him. ²⁶It had been revealed to him by the holy Spirit that he should not see death before he had seen the Messiah of the Lord. ²⁷He came in the Spirit into the temple; and when the parents brought in the child Jesus to perform the custom of the law in regard to him, ²⁸he took him into his arms and blessed God, saying:

> ²⁹"Now, Master, you may let your servant go
> in peace, according to your word,
> ³⁰for my eyes have seen your salvation,
> ³¹which you prepared in sight of all the peoples,
> ³²a light for revelation to the Gentiles,
> and glory for your people Israel."

³³The child's father and mother were amazed at what was said about him; ³⁴and Simeon blessed them and said to Mary his mother, "Behold, this child is destined for the fall and rise of

---

faithful, law-abiding Jews, and with them, Luke underscores the Jewish context of Jesus' birth and mission.

Nothing else is known about the identities of Simeon and Anna other than what this section tells us. Both represent the faithful Israelite who waits and does not lose hope in the coming redemption. Simeon's canticle, or *Nunc dimitiis* (2:29-32), is the fourth and final hymn from the Lukan infancy narratives and has traditionally been part of Compline or night office in the Liturgy of the Hours.

Simeon's words to Mary, ominous though they are, are also highly theological. With verse 34 we see the first instance of the schism motif, which runs throughout Luke's Gospel. Often in Luke's portrayal of Jesus' mission, one party or person will follow him, while another will turn away. One group will be saved, another will fall into perdition. In each case individuals choose their own fate by deciding for or against following Jesus. Simeon states that a sword will pierce Mary's heart as well. The discipleship that Jesus demands extends even to his mother. Not only does Luke indicate through Simeon that discipleship will not be easy, but he also elevates Mary to the role of the model disciple. To love Jesus is to suffer with him.

many in Israel, and to be a sign that will be contradicted [35](and yourself a sword will pierce) so that the thoughts of many hearts may be revealed." [36]There was also a prophetess, Anna, the daughter of Phanuel, of the tribe of Asher. She was advanced in years, having lived seven years with her husband after her marriage, [37]and then as a widow until she was eighty-four. She never left the temple, but worshiped night and day with fasting and prayer. [38]And coming forward at that very time, she gave thanks to God and spoke about the child to all who were awaiting the redemption of Jerusalem.

The Return to Nazareth. [39]When they had fulfilled all the prescriptions of the law of the Lord, they returned to

---

The widowed state of the prophetess Anna, daughter of Phanuel (vv. 36-38), has made her utterly dependent on God's goodness. Luke tells us that she "spoke about the child to all who were awaiting the redemption of Jerusalem" (v. 38), and thus she is the first evangelist. By starting out with the "redemption of Jerusalem," Luke sets his literary project in order. After the resurrection, the message goes from "Jerusalem, throughout Judea and Samaria, and to the ends of the earth" (Acts 1:8).

2:39-40 Nazareth and Bethlehem

According to the accounts of both Luke and Matthew, Jesus is born in Bethlehem but spends his youth and young adulthood in Nazareth. Mention of these two locales in this manner forms an enigmatic knot that is difficult to unravel. If there are serious questions surrounding the census (see 2:1-7 above), why do Mary and Joseph go to Bethlehem, when we know that Mary is from Nazareth (1:26)? The four Gospels and the Acts of the Apostles refer to "Jesus of Nazareth" but never "Jesus of Bethlehem." Is the whole narrative of the birth at Bethlehem a literary construction serving to demonstrate that Jesus, through his foster father Joseph, is the Son of David who is born in the city of David?

Scripture, history, and archaeology all show that there was a strong Jewish presence in various parts of Galilee, so it would not be a strange place for Jesus to have his upbringing. The most we can say about this puzzlement is that the two sources that mention Jesus' birth, Luke and Matthew, both specifically state that it occurs in Bethlehem. There are no texts that cite Nazareth as Jesus' birthplace. Basing their respective accounts on the oral tradition, the evangelists composed stories that get Mary and Joseph to Bethlehem and then back up to Nazareth. The importance of this Lukan narrative is that Jesus stands in line of the Davidic

Galilee, to their own town of Nazareth. [40]The child grew and became strong, filled with wisdom; and the favor of God was upon him.

The Boy Jesus in the Temple. [41]Each year his parents went to Jerusalem for the feast of Passover, [42]and when he was twelve years old, they went up according to festival custom. [43]After they had completed its days, as they were returning, the boy Jesus remained behind in Jerusalem, but his parents did not know it. [44]Thinking that he was in the caravan, they journeyed for a day and looked for him among their relatives and acquaintances, [45]but not finding him, they returned to Jerusalem to look for him. [46]After three days they found him in the temple, sitting in the midst of the teachers, listening to them and asking them questions, [47]and all who heard him were astounded at his understanding and his answers. [48]When his parents saw him, they were astonished, and his mother said to him, "Son, why have you done this to us? Your father and I have been looking for you with great anxiety." [49]And he said to them, "Why were you looking for me? Did you not know that I must be in my Father's house?" [50]But they did not understand what he said to them. [51]He went down with them and came to Nazareth, and was obedient to them; and his mother kept all these things in her heart. [52]And Jesus advanced [in] wisdom and age and favor before God and man.

Messiah, and about that, Luke wants the reader to know, there can be no doubt.

2:41-52 The boy Jesus in the temple

Only Luke contains this story of how Jesus is lost while on the return trip from Jerusalem. Passover was one of the pilgrimage feasts, when devout Jews would go to Jerusalem to celebrate the occasion.

The story itself reflects a theological point that Luke makes explicit in recounting Jesus' earthly ministry: true discipleship goes beyond familial relationships (8:19-21 and 11:27-29). In addition, that this conversation takes place in the temple reflects Luke's ambivalent attitude toward the temple's existence, if not his positive disposition toward it. Luke frequently shows Jesus teaching in the temple up to the final days before his crucifixion. In the Acts of the Apostles, Peter and Paul also preach and teach in the temple.

Jesus returns with his parents to Nazareth, and nothing more is heard about him until he is an adult and begins his ministry. The next time we read of Jesus in Jerusalem will be at his triumphal entry (19:28-39), which leads to his death.

III. The Preparation for the Public Ministry

3 **The Preaching of John the Baptist.** ¹In the fifteenth year of the reign of Tiberius Caesar, when Pontius Pilate was governor of Judea, and Herod was tetrarch of Galilee, and his brother Philip tetrarch of the region of Ituraea and Trachonitis, and Lysanias was tetrarch of Abilene, ²during the high priesthood of Annas and Caiaphas, the word of God came to John the son of Zechariah in the desert. ³He went throughout [the] whole region of the Jordan, proclaiming a baptism of repentance for the forgiveness of sins, ⁴as it is written in the book of the words of the prophet Isaiah:

THE PREPARATION FOR THE PUBLIC MINISTRY

Luke 3:1–4:13

John the Baptist is the precursor of Jesus, and Luke shifts the focus from one ministry to the other. This transition entails Jesus' baptism and desert temptation.

3:1-20 The ministry of John the Baptist

Chapter 3, like chapter 1, opens with a periodic sentence, a strong indication that this section is a major literary unit.

As with the birth of Jesus (Luke 2:1-3), Luke situates John the Baptist within a geopolitical framework involving the Roman emperor and his Palestinian-Jewish client states. Tiberius Caesar succeeds Augustus. According to Luke's dating, the word of God comes to the desert-dwelling John the Baptist in A.D. 29.

The nominally Jewish king, Herod the Great, died in 4 B.C. and divided his kingdom among his three sons: Herod Antipas, the tetrarch, or ruler, of Galilee and Perea; Herod Archelaus, ethnarch over Judea, Idumea, and Samaria; and Herod Philip, the tetrarch in charge of Gaulanitis, Trachonitis, and Batanaea. Archelaus's misrule led the emperor Augustus to banish him in A.D. 6, at which time a Roman procurator was appointed to govern his territory. One such procurator was Pontius Pilate, who ruled the area from A.D. 26 to 36, the period Luke is writing about here.

Lysanias is difficult to identify. There is scant information about a person of that name ruling the area of Abilene at this time. Many have speculated on the reason why Luke includes this information. Was he addressing a Christian community based in Abilene (northwest of Damascus), or was he from Abilene himself? We may never know, but we have

"A voice of one crying out in the
desert:
'Prepare the way of the Lord,
make straight his paths.
⁵Every valley shall be filled
and every mountain and hill
shall be made low.
The winding roads shall be made
straight,
and the rough ways made
smooth,
⁶and all flesh shall see the salvation
of God.'"

⁷He said to the crowds who came out
to be baptized by him, "You brood of
vipers! Who warned you to flee from the
coming wrath? ⁸Produce good fruits as
evidence of your repentance; and do not
begin to say to yourselves, 'We have
Abraham as our father,' for I tell you,
God can raise up children to Abraham
from these stones. ⁹Even now the ax lies
at the root of the trees. Therefore every
tree that does not produce good fruit will
be cut down and thrown into the fire."

here a typical example of the manner in which Luke uses historical data—
truth is more important than mere fact.

With the mention of high priests, Annas and Caiaphas, Luke grounds
the Baptist's ministry within the history of Jewish Palestine. From John's
Gospel (11:49; 18:13), we read that Caiaphas is the priest at the time of
Jesus' death. Although only one high priest ruled at a time, Luke may include the reference to Annas simply because Annas was still alive while
his son Caiaphas was in charge.

John the Baptist begins the public ministry in the parallel accounts of the
other three Gospels as well, but just where John preaches is a question.
Mark simply says "in the desert" (1:4). Matthew states "in the desert of
Judea" (3:1), which would place him under the jurisdiction of Pontius Pilate. Further on, both Matthew and Mark add that crowds come from Judea
and Jerusalem, a region accessible to Perea and Herod Antipas's territory.
Luke writes "in the desert . . . [the] whole region of the Jordan" (vv. 2-3), a
reading that suggests along the Jordan River, including the Judean side of
the river (Roman territory), but in any case, in that area east of Jerusalem as
far as the mountains on the east bank. Since Galilee is also under Herod Antipas, Luke seems to introduce the idea that both Jesus and John, each in his
proper time, face the same political ruler (see 3:19ff. and 23:6-12).

Luke firmly establishes John as the precursor. Not only does John
preach a baptism of repentance for the forgiveness of sins, but the evangelist (vv. 4-6) also interprets the Baptist's role as the fulfillment of Isaiah's
prophecy (40:3-5).

Judaism, with its whole tradition of the *mikvah,* or ritual bath, was well
acquainted with the water ablutions that John mentions (v. 16). The reference to a baptism "with the holy Spirit and fire" further on in the verse

25

The Jordan River, possibly near the site of Jesus' baptism

◄ ◄ ¹⁰And the crowds asked him, "What then should we do?" ¹¹He said to them in reply, "Whoever has two cloaks should share with the person who has none. And whoever has food should do likewise." ¹²Even tax collectors came to be baptized and they said to him, "Teacher, what should we do?" ¹³He answered them, "Stop collecting more than what is prescribed." ¹⁴Soldiers also asked him, "And what is it that we should do?" He told them, "Do not practice extortion, do not falsely accuse anyone, and be satisfied with your wages."

¹⁵Now the people were filled with expectation, and all were asking in their hearts whether John might be the Messiah. ◄ ¹⁶John answered them all, saying, "I am baptizing you with water, but one mightier than I is coming. I am not worthy to loosen the thongs of his sandals. He will baptize you with the holy Spirit and fire. ¹⁷His winnowing fan is in his hand to clear his threshing floor and to gather the wheat into his barn, but the chaff he will burn with unquenchable fire." ¹⁸Exhorting them in many other ways, he preached good news to the people. ¹⁹Now Herod the tetrarch, who had been censured by him because of Herodias, his brother's wife, and because of all the evil deeds Herod had committed, ²⁰added still another to these by [also] putting John in prison.

The Baptism of Jesus. ²¹After all the ► people had been baptized and Jesus

---

emphasizes that Jesus' action goes beyond religious ritual; it will have an efficacy that will transform the whole created order, just as fire alters the material state of matter. Early Christian mosaics depict this point by presenting Jesus standing in the Jordan River with smiling fish surrounding his feet as the Baptist pours water over Jesus' head.

3:21-22 The baptism of Jesus

John clarifies his subservient role to Christ with his preaching in 3:15-18. From the beginning of Luke's Gospel, information about John the Baptist has come before the accounts dealing with Jesus. In keeping with this thematic development of the Baptist as precursor, Luke skillfully provides the account of John's arrest (3:19-20) before the narrative surrounding Jesus' baptism (3:21-22).

Luke shows Jesus praying at critical points in his life. To underscore the point that John is lesser than Jesus, Luke recounts the baptism itself in the passive voice. There is no conversation between the two individuals. Jesus is baptized as one among the crowd, the voice from heaven is directed only to him, and it is understood that the others do not hear it. Later, when the Baptist sends messengers to Jesus (7:18-23), there is no indication of his being aware of having baptized Jesus.

To interpret the baptism, Luke relies on a conflation of two Old Testament passages. The first half of the voice from heaven (v. 22) is a paraphrase

also had been baptized and was praying, heaven was opened ²²and the holy Spirit descended upon him in bodily form like a dove. And a voice came from heaven, "You are my beloved Son; with you I am well pleased."

The Genealogy of Jesus. ²³When Jesus began his ministry he was about thirty years of age. He was the son, as was thought, of Joseph, the son of Heli,

²⁴the son of Matthat, the son of Levi, the son of Melchi, the son of Jannai, the son of Joseph, ²⁵the son of Mattathias, the son of Amos, the son of Nahum, the son of Esli, the son of Naggai, ²⁶the son of Maath, the son of Mattathias, the son of Semein, the son of Josech, the son of Joda, ²⁷the son of Joanan, the son of Rhesa, the son of Zerubbabel, the son of Shealtiel, the son of Neri, ²⁸the son of

of Psalm 2:7, while the second half is part of Isaiah 42:1. It should be noted, however, that the textual witnesses for this section display a wide variety of readings. One manuscript, for example, quotes Psalm 2:7 in its entirety: "You are my Son, this day I have begotten you." The version that we have here reflects the evidence from Codices Vaticanus and Sinaiticus, two of the most dependable of the extant Gospel manuscripts. A similar, although not an exact, quotation is found at the transfiguration of Jesus (9:35).

According to the science of the ancients, doves were considered not to have any bile and thus were symbolic of virtue. Not only were they worthy for sacrifice to God, but, as seen here, they also symbolized the divine presence.

3:23-38 The genealogy of Jesus

By setting Jesus' genealogy after the baptism, Luke fashions a twofold theological statement. First, after having seen Jesus' divine sonship pronounced in the voice from heaven (3:22), he now reiterates that point by stating it in verse 38. Second, Luke writes Jesus' ancestral line going all the way back to Adam, and by so doing connects Jesus to all humanity, unlike Matthew, who shows Jesus as descended from Abraham to stress his Jewish background and role (Matt 1:1-17). Luke also underscores Jesus' virginal conception by the use of the parenthetical expression "as was thought" (v. 23).

One theory of the formation of Luke's Gospel holds that the infancy narratives (Luke 1–2) were later additions to a primitive version of the current text (see above). If so, an earlier stage of the Third Gospel began with Jesus' baptism and genealogy. Supporting this possibility is a lack of similar introductory material in the other Gospels (Matthew notwithstanding), as well as use of Luke's Gospel by early Christians and heretics, particularly Marcion, who denied Christ's relationship with anyone in the Old

Melchi, the son of Addi, the son of
Cosam, the son of Elmadam, the son
of Er, ²⁹the son of Joshua, the son of
Eliezer, the son of Jorim, the son of
Matthat, the son of Levi, ³⁰the son of Si-
meon, the son of Judah, the son of
Joseph, the son of Jonam, the son of Eli-
akim, ³¹the son of Melea, the son of
Menna, the son of Mattatha, the son
of Nathan, the son of David, ³²the son

of Jesse, the son of Obed, the son of
Boaz, the son of Sala, the son of Nah-
shon, ³³the son of Amminadab, the son
of Admin, the son of Arni, the son of
Hezron, the son of Perez, the son of
Judah, ³⁴the son of Jacob, the son of Isaac,
the son of Abraham, the son of Terah,
the son of Nahor, ³⁵the son of Serug, the
son of Reu, the son of Peleg, the son of
Eber, the son of Shelah, ³⁶the son of

Testament. In any case, in this final redaction Luke does a fine job linking the first two chapters to the third both literarily and theologically.

4:1-13 The temptation in the desert

The Spirit who descended upon Jesus at his baptism now leads him into the desert for forty days.

The desert brings life right to the edge. In the Jewish tradition, it can be a place of divine encounter, such as with Moses and the burning bush (Exod 3:1-14), or it can be the place of death (see Gen 21:14-16). Of course, the forty-year wandering of the Israelites, a communal experience that formed them into the people of God, takes place in the desert. Just so, Jesus' sojourn in the wilderness brings into clearer focus for him what his mission on earth will be.

The Synoptic Gospels all include the desert temptation, but there are differences among them in the telling. Mark's account is the shortest (1:12-13), and Luke's is most similar to Matthew's (4:1-11), but the similarities break down in the respective nuances of each account. In Matthew, the setting of the three temptations goes from the desert, to Jerusalem, to the kingdoms of the world, while in Luke we read desert, kingdoms of the world, Jerusalem. Luke's account has greater internal consistency, for Jesus' ministry will culminate in Jerusalem, and it will be in that city that he meets his greatest temptation as well as his greatest triumph (see below, Luke 22:39-46; 23:44-49; 24). As it stands in this passage, the three temptations are to riches, glory, and power, represented by bread, rule, and defiance of nature respectively. Jesus' reply to each of the temptations, all from the book of Deuteronomy (8:3; 6:13, 16), connects his experience in the desert with that of the wandering Israelites.

For Luke, the devil is a force in the yet unredeemed world of Jesus' ministry. In the Lukan narrative, this encounter in the desert is Jesus' first

Cainan, the son of Arphaxad, the son of Shem, the son of Noah, the son of Lamech, ³⁷the son of Methuselah, the son of Enoch, the son of Jared, the son of Mahalaleel, the son of Cainan, ³⁸the son of Enos, the son of Seth, the son of Adam, the son of God.

4 **The Temptation of Jesus.** ¹Filled with the holy Spirit, Jesus returned from the Jordan and was led by the Spirit into the desert ²for forty days, to be tempted by the devil. He ate nothing during those days, and when they were over he was hungry. ³The devil said to him, "If you are the Son of God, command this stone to become bread." ⁴Jesus answered him, "It is written, 'One does not live by bread alone.'"

⁵Then he took him up and showed him all the kingdoms of the world in a single instant. ⁶The devil said to him, "I shall give to you all this power and their glory; for it has been handed over to me, and I may give it to whomever I wish. ⁷All this will be yours, if you worship me." ⁸Jesus said to him in reply, "It is written:

'You shall worship the Lord, your God,
and him alone shall you serve.'"

⁹Then he led him to Jerusalem, made him stand on the parapet of the temple, and said to him, "If you are the Son of God, throw yourself down from here, ¹⁰for it is written:

'He will command his angels concerning you,
to guard you,'

¹¹and:

'With their hands they will support you,
lest you dash your foot against a stone.'"

¹²Jesus said to him in reply, "It also says, 'You shall not put the Lord, your God, to the test.'" ¹³When the devil had finished every temptation, he departed from him for a time.

IV. The Ministry in Galilee

The Beginning of the Galilean Ministry. ¹⁴Jesus returned to Galilee in

---

meeting with the devil, but certainly not the last (v. 13). Jesus will be in hard combat with the devil or Satan from here until his death.

THE MINISTRY IN GALILEE

Luke 4:14–9:50

The Spirit now leads Jesus to Galilee, the area north of Jerusalem and Samaria. This was the district of his upbringing, and he begins his earthly ministry there.

4:14-30 Jesus arrives in Nazareth

From the preceding section we know that Jesus was away from the region and his hometown. What is unclear, however, is how long he was

the power of the Spirit, and news of him spread throughout the whole region. [15]He taught in their synagogues and was praised by all.

The Rejection at Nazareth. [16]He came to Nazareth, where he had grown up, and went according to his custom into the synagogue on the sabbath day. He stood up to read [17]and was handed a scroll of the prophet Isaiah. He unrolled the scroll and found the passage where it was written:

[18]"The Spirit of the Lord is upon me,
because he has anointed me
to bring glad tidings to the poor.

He has sent me to proclaim liberty to captives
and recovery of sight to the blind,
to let the oppressed go free,
[19]and to proclaim a year acceptable to the Lord."

[20]Rolling up the scroll, he handed it back to the attendant and sat down, and the eyes of all in the synagogue looked intently at him. [21]He said to them, "Today this scripture passage is fulfilled in your hearing." [22]And all spoke highly of him and were amazed at the gracious words that came from his mouth. They also asked, "Isn't this the son of Joseph?" [23]He said to them,

---

away and why he departed. That he was baptized with all the people somewhere along the Jordan (3:3, 21) has led many to conclude that Jesus was associated with John the Baptist for some time before setting out on his own way.

Jesus reads from Isaiah 61:1-2, a messianic text. Although by the fourth century A.D. the rabbis had adopted a particular order of scriptural pericopes to be read throughout the year, it is uncertain whether such a system was in place in first-century Judaism. If it was, then Jesus demonstrates his authority in bypassing the accepted practice and choosing a passage of his own. His concluding comment (v. 21) allows the listeners to draw their own conclusions.

The reaction of the people in Nazareth reflects the schism motif, which Luke develops from the beginning (see 2:34). Some speak highly of Jesus, while others are filled with resentment at having one of their own preach to them, and Jesus calls them on this point by providing examples from their history when the people acted in like manner. The references to Elijah and Elisha serve to describe the kind of prophet people see in Jesus and, indeed, how he perhaps sees himself. Unlike the prophets of the south, such as Isaiah and Jeremiah, Elijah and Elisha lived in the north, and they, too, made the rounds raising the dead, feeding the poor, and healing the sick (1 Kgs 17:1–2 Kgs 13). Since Galilee is in the north, where much of Jesus' ministry is situated, both the actions and words of Jesus

"Surely you will quote me this proverb, 'Physician, cure yourself,' and say, 'Do here in your native place the things that we heard were done in Capernaum.'" ²⁴And he said, "Amen, I say to you, no prophet is accepted in his own native place. ²⁵Indeed, I tell you, there were many widows in Israel in the days of Elijah when the sky was closed for three and a half years and a severe famine spread over the entire land. ²⁶It was to none of these that Elijah was sent, but only to a widow in Zarephath in the land of Sidon. ²⁷Again, there were many lepers in Israel during the time of Elisha the prophet; yet not one of them was cleansed, but only Naa-man the Syrian." ²⁸When the people in the synagogue heard this, they were all filled with fury. ²⁹They rose up, drove him out of the town, and led him to the brow of the hill on which their town had been built, to hurl him down head-long. ³⁰But he passed through the midst of them and went away.

The Cure of a Demoniac. ³¹Jesus then went down to Capernaum, a town of Galilee. He taught them on the sabbath, ³²and they were astonished at his teaching because he spoke with authority. ³³In the synagogue there was a man with the spirit of an unclean demon, and he cried out in a loud voice, ³⁴"Ha! What have you to do with us, Jesus of

would have special resonance with the people. Jesus' comments draw the obvious conclusion. By their resistance to him, the townspeople are no better than their forebears who did not heed earlier prophets; therefore, they come under the same judgment. Jesus' insinuation enrages the people to the point where they try to kill him.

Nazareth is located on a hill overlooking the Esdraelon Plain. A rocky precipice encircles the southeast section of the town.

4:31-44 Exorcisms, cures, and healings at Capernaum

The central focus of Jesus' ministry is the reclamation of this world for the reign of God, and now the battle begins.

Capernaum lies along the northern shore of the Sea of Galilee, where archaeological evidence points to its being a busy fishing village. Much of Jesus' ministry takes place in this locale.

Unlike the temptation scene in Luke 4:1-13, here Jesus encounters not the devil but an unclean demon. For Luke, both the demon and the devil may represent the same evil force, but they are not one and the same entities. The devil, Satan, and Beelzebul (see 10:18; 11:14-23) are synonymous terms for the Evil One holding creation captive. Demons, on the other hand, play a lesser role and are subject to the devil. That this exorcism as well as the following cure takes place on the sabbath is significant: the reign of God is made manifest on the literal day of the Lord, which,

Nazareth? Have you come to destroy us? I know who you are—the Holy One of God!" ³⁵Jesus rebuked him and said, "Be quiet! Come out of him!" Then the demon threw the man down in front of them and came out of him without doing him any harm. ³⁶They were all amazed and said to one another, "What is there about his word? For with authority and power he commands the unclean spirits, and they come out." ³⁷And news of him spread everywhere in the surrounding region.

The Cure of Simon's Mother-in-Law. ³⁸After he left the synagogue, he entered the house of Simon. Simon's mother-in-law was afflicted with a severe fever, and they interceded with him about her. ³⁹He stood over her, rebuked the fever, and it left her. She got up immediately and waited on them.

Other Healings. ⁴⁰At sunset, all who had people sick with various diseases brought them to him. He laid his hands on each of them and cured them. ⁴¹And demons also came out from many,

---

metaphorically speaking, is the *Day of the Lord*, the moment when the end times arrive culminating in the Lord's decisive battle with evil. When the Gospels were written, apocalyptic thought filled the thoughts of Jew and Gentile alike, and this Lukan scene reflects such a mindset. The Gospels are in a large way responsible for the fact that judgment of good and evil is an important part of the Christian theological tradition.

The cure of Simon's mother-in-law follows. The world between sickness, disease, and demonic possession was not so well defined in ancient times. None of it was good, and all of it was evil. Curing a person, therefore, would evoke the same reaction as an exorcism, a point made by the fact that Jesus "rebukes" the fever. Again, the event takes place on the sabbath, leading to the same conclusions as above. From earliest Christianity, a house located in the center of Capernaum has been held as the place of veneration commemorating this miracle, and churches have stood on the spot ever since to accommodate the thousands of pilgrims who continue to visit it.

The sabbath ends at sunset, yet people still come to Jesus for cures and exorcisms. The day of the Lord cannot be confined to the temporal cycle. The passage shows the melding of time with the *eschaton*. The demons always know Jesus' identity, even though the people do not, and these unclean spirits nearly always declare him the Messiah or state his divinity. Jesus prohibits them from speaking in order to demonstrate his power over them and their ruler, the devil.

Jesus leaves Capernaum at daybreak and goes to a deserted place. Tradition has often located this spot along the northeast shore of the Sea of

Fishermen docked in the harbor at Jaffa along the Mediterranean coast

shouting, "You are the Son of God." But he rebuked them and did not allow them to speak because they knew that he was the Messiah.

Jesus Leaves Capernaum. ⁴²At daybreak, Jesus left and went to a deserted place. The crowds went looking for him, and when they came to him, they tried to prevent him from leaving them. ⁴³But he said to them, "To the other towns also I must proclaim the good news of the kingdom of God, because for this purpose I have been sent."

⁴⁴And he was preaching in the synagogues of Judea.

5 The Call of Simon the Fisherman. ¹While the crowd was pressing in on Jesus and listening to the word of God, he was standing by the Lake of Gennesaret. ²He saw two boats there alongside the lake; the fishermen had disembarked and were washing their nets. ³Getting into one of the boats, the one belonging to Simon, he asked him to put out a short distance from the shore. Then he sat down and taught the

---

Galilee, a place of volcanic rock and little vegetation. Luke, not known for his accuracy in Palestinian geography, ends the section by saying that Jesus goes to preach in the synagogues of Judea. This point of information is problematic. Judea is in the south. Luke's whole schema has Jesus making only one trip there, and it ends with his passion, death, and resurrection. The earliest manuscripts, Codices Sinaiticus and Vaticanus read "Judea," but another important codex has "Galilee," the district in the north, probably written thus to resolve the narrative contradiction. Most likely Jesus made more than one journey to Judea in his lifetime. Indeed, John's Gospel indicates that Jesus went to Jerusalem at least seven times. This verse (v. 44) reflects such a tradition.

5:1-11 The miraculous draft of fish and the call of Peter

Luke is the only Synoptic writer to include the story of the miraculous catch of fish within the call of Simon, although John's Gospel shows a similar miracle in a resurrection narrative (John 21:1-11).

Lake of Gennesaret is another name for Sea of Galilee (v. 1). Fishing in the Sea of Galilee is done only at night. If the men caught nothing at that time, there was nothing to be had. That they listened to Jesus at all is indicative that they respected Jesus' opinion even when it came to their own profession. There is a tinge of doubt in Simon's reply (v. 5), and his reaction only confirms his initial skepticism (v. 8).

Jesus speaks only to Simon, and Simon is the only one to reply. Luke is preparing the reader for the leadership role that Simon (Peter) will play throughout the Lukan corpus. We get the impression that the crowd must have been so large that the only way Jesus could be seen and heard without

crowds from the boat. ⁴After he had finished speaking, he said to Simon, "Put out into deep water and lower your nets for a catch." ⁵Simon said in reply, "Master, we have worked hard all night and have caught nothing, but at your command I will lower the nets." ⁶When they had done this, they caught a great number of fish and their nets were tearing. ⁷They signaled to their partners in the other boat to come to help them. They came and filled both boats so that they were in danger of sinking. ⁸When Simon Peter saw this, he fell at the knees of Jesus and said, "Depart from me, Lord, for I am a sinful man." ⁹For astonishment at the catch of fish they had made seized him and all those with him, ¹⁰and likewise James and John, the sons of Zebedee, who were partners of Simon. Jesus said to Simon, "Do not be afraid; from now on you will be catching men." ¹¹When they brought their boats to the shore, they left everything and followed him.

The Cleansing of the Leper. ¹²Now there was a man full of leprosy in one of the towns where he was; and when he saw Jesus, he fell prostrate, pleaded with him, and said, "Lord, if you wish, you can make me clean." ¹³Jesus stretched out his hand, touched him,

being overwhelmed by the throng was to sit in Simon's boat just off the beach, the same boat that sails out for the catch at the Lord's command. The emphasis on Simon's boat is Luke's way of underscoring the disciple's importance on the symbolic level. Early Christian iconography often used a boat filled with people to depict the church, just as the church has long been called the "bark of Peter."

The miracle excites awe and wonder. Moreover, it represents the multitudinous followers this disciple will "catch" once he becomes a fisher of people in Christ's name. In verse 8 Luke uses the name "Simon Peter" for the only time and shows the disciple moved to repentance. Jesus then speaks directly to Simon in listening distance of the others. Jesus' call results in these fishermen responding immediately. They leave everything and follow, thereby becoming models of the perfect disciples.

5:12-16 The cleansing of a leper

In the Old and New Testaments, the term "leprosy" is used to describe a variety of skin diseases, including leprosy itself. Any skin abnormalities, particularly those ulcerating or scabbing, made ritual purity impossible. Whether or not the disease was contagious, the affliction was considered a sign of sinfulness, and so people so afflicted were separated from the community to prevent physical as well as cultic contamination. After viewing the symptoms of the disease, the priests made the determination on purity or impurity (see Lev 13–14).

and said, "I do will it. Be made clean." And the leprosy left him immediately. [14]Then he ordered him not to tell anyone, but "Go, show yourself to the priest and offer for your cleansing what Moses prescribed; that will be proof for them." [15]The report about him spread all the more, and great crowds assembled to listen to him and to be cured of their ailments, [16]but he would withdraw to deserted places to pray.

The Healing of a Paralytic. [17]One day as Jesus was teaching, Pharisees and teachers of the law were sitting there who had come from every village of Galilee and Judea and Jerusalem, and the power of the Lord was with him for healing. [18]And some men brought on a stretcher a man who was paralyzed; they were trying to bring him in and set [him] in his presence. [19]But not finding a way to bring him in because of the crowd, they went up on the roof and lowered him on the stretcher through the tiles into the middle in front of Jesus. [20]When he saw their faith, he said, "As for you, your sins are forgiven." [21]Then the scribes and Pharisees began to ask themselves, "Who is this who speaks blasphemies? Who but God alone can forgive sins?" [22]Jesus knew their thoughts and said to them in reply, "What are you thinking in your hearts? [23]Which is easier, to say,

---

The man prostrates himself and acknowledges Jesus' authority both by the title "Lord" and by the supplication "if you wish" (v. 12). His action shows his faith, which Jesus recognizes. Jesus' commanding the cleansing is an affirmation of his lordship. The injunction not to tell anyone echoes the messianic secret found in much of the Gospel of Mark. Of course, it would be impossible to keep. It shows, however, that Jesus prefers that his actions rather than his words speak of his reign. Indeed, Jesus relies on such actions as proof of his being the Messiah (Luke 7:22). As a means of evangelization, the cure has the desired affect of bringing others to Jesus. Rather than portraying Jesus as being another miracle worker among many, Luke notes that the crowds assembled first "to listen to him." Only then were they "cured of their ailments" (v. 15).

Luke, more than any other evangelist, frequently shows Jesus alone at prayer, an activity hinted at in Luke 4:42. Often Jesus retreats to a deserted place or wilderness after an intense period of preaching, healing, and exorcising, as he does here.

5:17-26 The healing of a paralytic

Although all three Synoptic Gospels have the healing of a paralytic, only Mark and Luke feature the bearers of the stretcher letting the person down through the roof. This story provides a number of details that describe the effect Jesus was having in his ministry.

'Your sins are forgiven,' or to say, 'Rise and walk'? [24]But that you may know that the Son of Man has authority on earth to forgive sins"—he said to the man who was paralyzed, "I say to you, rise, pick up your stretcher, and go home." [25]He stood up immediately before them, picked up what he had been lying on, and went home, glorifying God. [26]Then astonishment seized them all and they glorified God, and, struck with awe, they said, "We have seen incredible things today."

The Call of Levi. [27]After this he went out and saw a tax collector named Levi sitting at the customs post. He said to him, "Follow me." [28]And leaving everything behind, he got up and followed him. [29]Then Levi gave a great banquet for him in his house, and a

---

The crowds he was able to draw must have been exceedingly large. The fact that Jesus teaches from a boat in Luke 5:3 gives us a hint of their size. In this passage the stretcher-bearers cannot possibly make their way through the people gathered in front of the door and must resort to unconventional methods.

Luke shows his Syrian origins here. The Markan parallel to this story says, "After they had broken through" (Mark 2:4), a statement describing better the roofs of Jewish homes in Palestine, which were flat and made of a mud-and-sod mixture resting on wooden beams or stone arches. These roofs often served as terraces on warm summer evenings. To maintain their impermeability during the rainy season, they would be rolled with a large rounded stone to compact the grasses. Burrowing a hole to let down a pallet would have been relatively easy. On the other hand, Luke states "through the tiles" (v. 19), a detail reflecting the domestic architecture stretching from the Golan Heights up into most of Syria, where a series of stone arches commonly support a roof made of shingles.

Although many see this passage as the first of several "conflict stories," there is no reason to conclude that the Pharisees and teachers of the Law are present with bad intentions, for there are no harsh words between them and Jesus until he forgives the paralytic's sins. The Pharisees are correct in their criticism—only God can forgive sins—but they do not know the full meaning of what they say. Jesus, referring to himself as the "Son of Man" for the first time in Luke (v. 24), proves his divinity with the cure, and everyone, including the Pharisees and teachers, is awestruck. Their attitude may change as Jesus progresses in his ministry, but at this point the tension is not evident. In line with the schism motif that Luke has developed (see Luke 2:34), this scene gives reason to believe that this group of Pharisees and scribes are convinced that Jesus does have such authority.

large crowd of tax collectors and others were at table with them. ³⁰The Pharisees and their scribes complained to his disciples, saying, "Why do you eat and drink with tax collectors and sinners?" ³¹Jesus said to them in reply, "Those who are healthy do not need a physician, but the sick do. ³²I have not come to call the righteous to repentance but sinners."

As an Aramaic phrase, the title "Son of Man" can be loosely translated by the pronoun "someone." It is used frequently in the Old Testament, especially in Ezekiel and Daniel. It gains specific import, however, in the latter book, which reads, "As the visions during the night continued, I saw One like a son of man coming, on the clouds of heaven; When he reached the Ancient One and was presented before him, He received dominion, glory, and kinship; nations and peoples of every language serve him. His dominion is an everlasting dominion that shall not be taken away, his kingship shall not be destroyed" (7:13-14). This quotation from Daniel is seminal for formation of the Christian understanding of Jesus' identity, and it is this reference, combined with the cure, which causes the crowd and the Pharisees to be awestruck. They are able to make the connection between the miracle and the person performing it.

The event itself is a good example of the incarnational character of Jesus' mission. Forgiveness of sins and spiritual well-being are not separated from physical wholeness and restoration. The Son of Man does not ignore the material world or the suffering of those living in it. By the double action of forgiving sins and curing the paralysis, Jesus shows that God's beloved creatures are redeemed in this life as well as the next.

5:27-32 The call of Levi, the tax collector

The Jewish people detested tax collectors for good reason. On the religious level, tax collectors made themselves idolaters by cooperating with the Romans; thus they at least tacitly acclaimed Caesar's lordship. Dealing with Roman coinage, which featured an engraving of the emperor, would support such an accusation. On the nationalistic plane, by working for the Romans, Jewish tax collectors betrayed their people. They received their positions by bidding themselves out as agents to the Roman State. The Romans assessed the sum a district should provide to the emperor; the Roman officials demanded a surcharge for themselves, and the collectors were bound to bring in both while taking any extra as their remuneration. They could and would sell whole families into slavery in order to meet their demands. This position made them extortionists, both symbolically and literally.

The Question about Fasting. [33]And they said to him, "The disciples of John fast often and offer prayers, and the disciples of the Pharisees do the same; but yours eat and drink." [34]Jesus answered them, "Can you make the wed-

---

All three Synoptic Gospels contain this story. Levi sits at the "customs post" (*telōnion* in Greek). This detail tells us that Levi taxed goods going from one political jurisdiction to another. Since nearly eighty percent of Jesus' ministry occurs along the northern shore of the Sea of Galilee, this customs post was most likely located at the mouth of the Jordan River, which formed the border between Galilee, under Herod Antipas, and Gaulanitis, under his brother Philip. The alacrity with which Levi leaves his post at the customs house indicates that his heart was predisposed to conversion before his encounter with Christ; Jesus' call is the catalyst causing the move toward repentance.

Levi's great banquet (*dochē* in Greek) with a large number of invitees underscores his wealth (v. 29). Luke's version differs from the Matthean (9:9-13) and Markan (2:13-17) accounts in several ways. Whereas the other two Synoptics specify that the Pharisees and scribes see Jesus in attendance and then speak to his disciples, Luke simply states that the Pharisees "complained" to his disciples, which leads one to believe that they were at the celebration. Were the Pharisees invited and only saw the rest of the company when they arrived? Would they have gone to a tax collector's banquet in the first place? Whatever the answer, Luke wants the reader to know that the Pharisees were in close proximity to Jesus. Unlike the preceding passage of the paralytic, where friction is not necessarily evident between Jesus and the Pharisees, here Luke describes the encounter between the two with the use of the Greek verb *gongyzō*, "to grumble against someone" or "complain," indicating that some visible tension has arisen between them (v. 30).

The parallel accounts in the other two Synoptics show "Matthew" and "Levi, son of Alphaeus" as the names of the tax collector, but Luke reads "Levi," a name suggesting that he comes from a Levitical family and therefore would have some kind of priestly function (see Deut 31:9; Josh 13:14). Certainly Luke could have shortened Mark's reading by dropping the identifier "son of Alphaeus." The name "Levi" itself, however, contains overtones of the impending messianic age.

In Malachi 3:3 we read, "and he will purify the sons of Levi, / Refining them like gold or like silver / that they may offer due sacrifice to the LORD." This prophet emphasizes the impending Day of the Lord as well as the point that a messenger will come to prepare the way (Mal 3:1). Luke gives

ding guests fast while the bridegroom is with them? ³⁵But the days will come, and when the bridegroom is taken away from them, then they will fast in those days." ³⁶And he also told them a parable. "No one tears a piece from a

---

attention to John the Baptist as well as to the Day of the Lord. That Levi leaves his functions at the customs post is a sign that this remarkable day has arrived. Hence the feast, which the now repentant Levi holds, prefigures the heavenly banquet. By calling this former tax collector to a new life, the Lord Jesus has purified the sons of Levi. Note as well that with this passage Luke has blended the ministries of the Baptist and Jesus.

5:33-39 Feasting and fasting, new and old

Comparing the three Synoptic versions of this story, we see that Matthew has the disciples of John the Baptist asking Jesus why his disciples do not fast (Matt 9:14). Mark has "people" inquiring, but with a reference to both John's disciples and the Pharisees (Mark 2:18). Luke is obviously editing material that has come through Mark. The antecedent of the pronoun "they" (Luke 5:33) is difficult to identify. Since further on in the verse there is mention of the Pharisees in the third person, "the disciples of the Pharisees do the same," it would seem that the scribes are asking the question. As a professional class of writers who knew the written law, they would not necessarily be as prone to follow the oral traditions promulgated by the Pharisees, even though they may have very well been aware of them.

In addition, the thematic content supports the scribes as the ones interrogating Jesus. This question about eating habits follows within the context of Levi's great banquet (Luke 5:27-32). A similar controversy over feasting and fasting arises further on in Jesus' ministry (Luke 7:31-35). It seems obvious that Jesus has developed a reputation for being one who enjoys good food and wine, and according to the Gospel account, this accusation is not without basis. Not only does he use banquet imagery in much of his preaching, but he is frequently seen at dinner feasts with Pharisees, tax collectors, and sinners. Indeed, Jesus refers to himself as a bridegroom in this passage, thus making his ministry on earth a wedding banquet filled with the joy and the promise of new life. It is the Day of the Lord.

This passage reflects the tensions existing between the Christian movement and Pharisaic Judaism. Although Luke goes to great lengths to demonstrate Christianity's roots in Jewish tradition, particularly in the

new cloak to patch an old one. Otherwise, he will tear the new and the piece from it will not match the old cloak. ³⁷Likewise, no one pours new wine into old wineskins. Otherwise, the new wine will burst the skins, and it will be spilled, and the skins will be ruined. ³⁸Rather, new wine must be poured into fresh wineskins. ³⁹[And] no one who has been drinking old wine desires new, for he says, 'The old is good.'"

6 **Debates about the Sabbath.** ¹While he was going through a field of grain on a sabbath, his disciples were picking the heads of grain, rubbing them in their hands, and eating them. ²Some Pharisees said, "Why are you doing what is unlawful on the sabbath?" ³Jesus said to them in reply, "Have you not read what David did when he and those [who were] with him were hungry? ⁴[How] he went into the

---

prophets (see Luke 1–2), the religious practices of the early Pharisees and Christians were incompatible. This irreconcilability stands as the background to the passage.

The parable about new and old patches, cloaks, and wineskins has a twist. The lesson about cloth and wineskins is easy to follow, and the conclusions are based on common sense. One uses old cloth to patch new, not vice versa; the fermentation of new wine needs the elasticity of new skins, not the brittleness of old ones. The summarizing statement, a verse that only Luke shows, however, is ironic: "[And] no one who has been drinking old wine desires new, for he says, 'The old is good'" (v. 39). After a discourse on the desirability of leaving the old for the new, Jesus concludes by admitting that we often prefer the comfort of the old to the challenges of the new, particularly when we see nothing wrong or bad with the old. On the other hand, the examination of the metaphor shows that, in this case, there is something wrong and bad about the old. Threadbare clothing is of little use to anyone, and wineskins can be used only once. We must not let comfort and security blind us to the blessings of the kingdom.

Jesus' point is that the life of a disciple is not a dour regimen of religious protocol, but a life of joy. We should not let self-complacency blind us to the banquet the Bridegroom has ushered in, a banquet that begins now even as we wait to see its fullness in the yet-to-come.

6:1-11 Debates about the sabbath

The Mosaic prohibition against work on the sabbath recurs in many places throughout the Pentateuch. The legislation first surfaces in Exodus 16:23-29, where Moses directs the Israelites on how to collect the manna the Lord has given them. They are to gather enough for the day at hand and leave none for the next day. This instruction is in force until the sixth

house of God, took the bread of offering, which only the priests could lawfully eat, ate of it, and shared it with his companions." ⁵Then he said to them, "The Son of Man is lord of the sabbath."

⁶On another sabbath he went into the synagogue and taught, and there was a man there whose right hand was withered. ⁷The scribes and the Pharisees watched him closely to see if he would cure on the sabbath so that they might discover a reason to accuse him. ⁸But he realized their intentions and said to the man with the withered hand, "Come up and stand before us." And he rose and stood there. ⁹Then Jesus said to them, "I ask you, is it lawful to do good on the sabbath rather than to do evil, to save life rather than to destroy it?" ¹⁰Looking around at them

day, when they are to gather twice as much for the following sabbath. Interestingly, when some disobey Moses by keeping some manna longer than they are supposed to, the cache becomes rotten and wormy. When the leftovers are saved for the sabbath, however, the manna remains edible. This Exodus account gives rise to further legislation and consequent debates on what constitutes work on the sabbath.

The controversy revolves around sabbath regulation. If the disciples performed a similar action on any other day of the week, they would have been within their rights (Deut 23:25). Here, however, not only are the disciples in Luke 6:1-5 violating prohibitions against harvesting fields and threshing grain, but by carrying goods, they are also guilty of breaking a sabbath law (see Num 15:32). Jesus' reply to the Pharisees is nearly the same in the other two Synoptic parallels (see Matt 12:1-8; Mark 2:23-28).

The incident to which Luke refers is found in 1 Samuel 21:1-7. Jesus' point is that Pharisees overlook David's infractions, who, with his men, is guilty of breaking more laws than the disciples are. Yet the Pharisees become indignant at Jesus for a less serious offense, and he is the Lord of the sabbath. This moment is one of messianic revelation, but the Pharisees' legalism blinds them to it. The passage ends with "The Son of Man is lord of the sabbath" (v. 5), a verse that introduces another story on violating the sabbath.

The issue at hand is not that Jesus cures but that he cures on the sabbath, something that is considered work. As with the exorcism of the demoniac (Luke 4:31-37), the sabbath or Lord's Day here is also considered the eschatological Day of the Lord, when suffering will cease and wholeness will be restored. Jesus tries to make that point when he addresses the assembly (v. 9), and he proves his lordship in restoring the man's withered hand (v. 10). Seeing that Jesus' argument and actions are unassailable, the scribes and Pharisees become incensed.

all, he then said to him, "Stretch out your hand." He did so and his hand was restored. ¹¹But they became enraged and discussed together what they might do to Jesus.

The Mission of the Twelve. ¹²In those days he departed to the mountain to pray, and he spent the night in prayer to God. ¹³When day came, he called his disciples to himself, and from them he chose Twelve, whom he also named apostles: ¹⁴Simon, whom he named Peter, and his brother Andrew, James, John, Philip, Bartholomew, ¹⁵Matthew, Thomas, James the son of Alphaeus, Simon who was called a Zealot, ¹⁶and Judas the son of James, and Judas Iscariot, who became a traitor.

Ministering to a Great Multitude. ¹⁷And he came down with them and

---

It is important to note that Jesus' conflicts with the Pharisees reflect more the tension within the early Christian community concerning Jews and Jewish practice than they do between Jesus and the Jews. Both Jews and Gentiles saw themselves as followers of Christ, and passages such as these show the points of contention both inside and outside the Christian community. Thus, when Jesus castigates the Pharisees in this passage, we see and hear the early debates within the Jewish-Christian community.

6:12-16 The mission of the Twelve

There is a noticeable shift of direction in this scene. Away from the synagogues, towns, and people, Jesus goes "to the mountain to pray" (v. 12) in an all-night vigil. The exact mountain is unknown, though the use of the definite article indicates that Lukan tradition must have had some specific mountain in mind. Galilee has many high places that could qualify as quiet retreats for prayer, but two are the most likely promontories: Mount Hermon, rising from the northeast corner of the Sea of Galilee, and Mount Tabor, south of the sea, visible from Nazareth and on the Jezreel Plain. They both have been traditional places of prayer from earliest antiquity (see Ps 89:13), although Tabor is the more accessible of the two.

Jesus selects from all his disciples twelve men who will have a share in his ministry. The names of the Twelve do not match the lists of the other Gospels, nor do they correspond with what Luke writes in his second volume (see Acts 1:13). In fact, none of the lists in the Synoptics are in exact agreement with each other. How do we account for the fact that the apostles (and only Luke and Matthew call these men apostles) differ, especially when the early church placed so much emphasis on apostolic foundation in determining whether a community was orthodox or that its writings should be included in the canon? One suggestion for the variety of names is that each Gospel writer is recalling the representative figures

43

stood on a stretch of level ground. A great crowd of his disciples and a large number of the people from all Judea and Jerusalem and the coastal region of Tyre and Sidon ¹⁸came to hear him and to be healed of their diseases; and even those who were tormented by unclean spirits were cured. ¹⁹Everyone in the crowd sought to touch him because power came forth from him and healed them all.

Sermon on the Plain. ²⁰And raising his eyes toward his disciples he said:

"Blessed are you who are poor,
for the kingdom of God is yours.
²¹Blessed are you who are now hungry,
for you will be satisfied.
Blessed are you who are now weeping,
for you will laugh.

---

peculiar to the community for which he is writing. These figures may have known or worked with one or more of what came to be called "the Twelve." All four Gospels agree that Judas Iscariot betrays Jesus, however.

After the night in prayer, Jesus returns to his ministry, except now the people come to him.

6:17-19 Ministering to a great multitude

The crowd's various lands of origin give the reader insight into Luke's geographical understanding as well as his theological agenda. The commission described in Acts 1:8 reads: "you will be my witnesses in Jerusalem, throughout Judea and Samaria, and to the ends of the earth." In the Acts of the Apostles, the apostolic mission follows that trajectory. Here in this passage, however, "Samaria" and the "ends of the earth" are not included. The explanation can be found in Luke 9:52-53, where Jesus and his disciples are not welcomed in the Samaritan village. Samaria's time will come, and so will the proclamation to the ends of the earth. For now, Tyre and Sidon, as seaports and in pagan territory, represent for Luke the future direction of the Christian movement. In this passage Luke paints a picture of a mission at the threshold.

6:20-49 Sermon on the Plain

The Sermon on the Plain evidences four sections: the Beatitudes, the exhortations, the analogy of trees and fruit, and the parable of the two houses.

Beatitudes. Jesus descends the mountain before preaching. The Moses typology, so much a part of Matthew's Gospel, does not exist in Luke. He raises his eyes towards his disciples, and addresses the people (v. 20), a simple gesture that calls forth discipleship on the part of the crowd. Because

²²Blessed are you when people hate you,
and when they exclude and insult you,
and denounce your name as evil on account of the Son of Man.

²³Rejoice and leap for joy on that day! Behold, your reward will be great in heaven. For their ancestors treated the prophets in the same way.

²⁴But woe to you who are rich,
for you have received your consolation.
²⁵But woe to you who are filled now,
for you will be hungry.
Woe to you who laugh now,
for you will grieve and weep.

²⁶Woe to you when all speak well of you,
for their ancestors treated the false prophets in this way.

Love of Enemies. ²⁷"But to you who hear I say, love your enemies, do good to those who hate you, ²⁸bless those who curse you, pray for those who mistreat you. ²⁹To the person who strikes you on one cheek, offer the other one as well, and from the person who takes your cloak, do not withhold even your tunic. ³⁰Give to everyone who asks of you, and from the one who takes what is yours do not demand it back. ³¹Do to others as you would have them do to you. ³²For if you love those who love

Luke has his Gentile audience in mind, he does not include the *lex talionis* found in Matthew 5:38. Certainly not as quoted or well known as Matthew's Beatitudes, the Lukan redaction is also shorter. Most critics believe that both Matthew and Luke use Q as the source material for their respective versions.

The great reversal theme, first outlined in the *Magnificat* (Luke 1:46-55), recurs here: the poor will inherit the kingdom, the hungry will be satisfied, those weeping will laugh. Luke addresses the people in the second person, whereas Matthew uses the third person. For this reason, some maintain that Luke foresees an immediate resolution to the suffering of the outcast while holding that Matthew pushes justice into the *eschaton*. The interpretation of the Lukan Beatitudes is not that simple, however. Because the Lukan eschatological vision surfaces through the juxtaposition of the Woes in verses 24-26, there is no reason to assume that Luke sees the resolution of the tension between the blessed and the woebegone occurring only within this lifetime. Likewise, Matthew's Beatitudes challenge people to address social injustices in this world.

Luke, like Matthew, places suffering and reward within the context of the Old Testament, in which true prophets faced torture and death, while the false ones found worldly grace and favor. As the Gospel narrative con-

you, what credit is that to you? Even sinners love those who love them. [33]And if you do good to those who do good to you, what credit is that to you? Even sinners do the same. [34]If you lend money to those from whom you expect repayment, what credit [is] that to you? Even sinners lend to sinners, and get back the same amount. [35]But rather, love your enemies and do good to them, and lend expecting nothing back; then your reward will be great and you will be children of the Most High, for he himself is kind to the ungrateful and the wicked. [36]Be merciful, just as [also] your Father is merciful.

Judging Others. [37]"Stop judging and you will not be judged. Stop condemning and you will not be condemned. Forgive and you will be forgiven. [38]Give and gifts will be given to you; a good measure, packed together, shaken down, and overflowing, will be poured into your lap. For the measure with which you measure will in return be measured out to you." [39]And he told them a parable, "Can a blind person guide a blind person? Will not both fall into a pit? [40]No disciple is superior to the teacher; but when fully trained, every disciple will be like his teacher. [41]Why do you notice the splinter in your brother's eye, but do not perceive the wooden beam in your own? [42]How can you say to your brother, 'Brother, let me remove that splinter in your

tinues, the reader sees Jesus encountering a similar fate. The heart of the message is that we do God's will on earth to relieve suffering and oppression, realizing all along that ultimate mercy and justice will come only with the *eschaton*.

Exhortations. Luke goes to great lengths in explaining love of enemies (vv. 27-38). Human love should match divine love, a love that is "kind to the ungrateful and the wicked" (v. 35). This call to be "merciful, just as [also] your Father is merciful" (v. 36) is a particular Lukan characteristic. Because Luke defines so well the boundless quality of divine mercy, Dante refers to the evangelist as the *Scritsa mansuetudinis Christi*, the "narrator of the sweet gentleness of Christ."

The lesson on judging others is connected to love of enemies. The context surrounding the admonition not to judge others does not refer to assessing the rightness or wrongness of an action or of its moral content; obviously, the whole of the Beatitudes contains elements of judgment. Rather, Luke is addressing those who would play the part of God by judging the salvation or damnation of others, something only God can do. For those who would assume to take on that role, Luke offers a stern warning: they may end up condemning themselves. Similarly, those who extend the benefit of the doubt will have manifold blessings extended to them (v. 38).

eye,' when you do not even notice the wooden beam in your own eye? You hypocrite! Remove the wooden beam from your eye first; then you will see clearly to remove the splinter in your brother's eye.

A Tree Known by Its Fruit. ⁴³"A good tree does not bear rotten fruit, nor does a rotten tree bear good fruit. ⁴⁴For every tree is known by its own fruit. For people do not pick figs from thornbushes, nor do they gather grapes from brambles. ⁴⁵A good person out of the store of goodness in his heart produces good, but an evil person out of a store of evil produces evil; for from the fullness of the heart the mouth speaks.

The Two Foundations. ⁴⁶"Why do you call me, 'Lord, Lord,' but not do what I command? ⁴⁷I will show you what someone is like who comes to me, listens to my words, and acts on them. ⁴⁸That one is like a person building a house, who dug deeply and laid the foundation on rock; when the flood came, the river burst against that house but could not shake it because it had been well built. ⁴⁹But the one who listens and does not act is like a person who built a house on the ground with-

Analogy. This comparison of a tree and its fruit is Q material. Matthew contains a nearly identical passage (Matt 7:16-20), but it is not as concise as the one we read here. The image of good and bad fruit and its association with prophecy echo several Old Testament prophetic utterances. Jeremiah performs an action of the good and bad figs (Jer 24:1-10), and a central metaphor for Isaiah (5:1-7) is the vine and grapes. Ezekiel has something similar (Ezek 19:10-14). Thus this short section functions as a reprise for Luke's reference to true and false prophets (vv. 23 and 26).

Parable. The comparison of the two houses (vv. 46-49; Matt 7:21-27) yields readings that reflect the geography of the two different communities. In Syria one would have to dig to reach the bedrock upon which to build; in Palestine and Israel, the bedrock is exposed. Syria has permanent rivers and streams running through it. Indeed, Antioch is situated on the Orontes, just one of several rivers in Syria. On the other hand, the country about which Matthew writes has only the Jordan, and no real city stands on its banks. The house for Matthew, therefore, is destroyed by wind and rain. The point in both readings, however, is the same: for one to follow Jesus, there must be care, determination, and full intention. The half-hearted who would try to be a disciple will simply wash away.

7:1-10 Healing the centurion's slave at Capernaum

Although Luke shares this story with Matthew, Luke's difference is most notable in that the evangelist includes the Jewish emissaries who are very supportive of the centurion. Several features draw our attention.

out a foundation. When the river burst against it, it collapsed at once and was completely destroyed."

7 The Healing of a Centurion's Slave.

¹When he had finished all his words to the people, he entered Capernaum. ²A centurion there had a slave who was ill and about to die, and he was valuable to him. ³When he heard about Jesus, he sent elders of the Jews to him, asking him to come and save the life of his slave. ⁴They approached Jesus and strongly urged him to come, saying, "He deserves to have you do this for him, ⁵for he loves our nation and he built the synagogue for us." ⁶And Jesus went with them, but when he was only a short distance from the house, the centurion sent friends to tell him, "Lord, do not trouble yourself, for I am not

---

The centurion, as the name implies, was in charge of one hundred men. At this time in history, Romans ruled the country through their clients, with Galilee and Perea under the jurisdiction of Herod Antipas. Hence the centurion need not have been a Roman, even though he was a Gentile. That he was a Gentile, however, would have entailed difficulties enough, for a Jew could not enter a Gentile home without becoming ritually impure.

There are two words in Greek used for the term "slave." One is *doulos,* and the other is *pais.* In verses 2, 3, 8, and 10, Luke uses *doulos,* and in verse 7 we read *pais.* Of the two words, the latter, which literally means, "boy" or "youth," describes a more personal, endearing relationship. On the other hand, *doulos* expresses the servility associated with such a state. The translation here, with its use of "slave" and "servant" in the respective verses, shows the nuance between the two words. Luke contrasts the two terms in the narrative. When using indirect address, as in verses 2, 3, and 10, or when the centurion speaks in the abstract, as in verse 8, the text shows *doulos.* When Luke quotes the centurion, however, he employs the term *pais.* From this juxtaposition we can see that Luke is emphasizing the kinship the centurion feels for his servant.

The interplay between the Jewish elders and the centurion is notable. Although the centurion is in service to the nominally Jewish tetrarch, Herod Antipas, he is still a Gentile. Herod Antipas, as a Roman client, has to pay tribute to the Romans, and he passes on this expense by levying heavy taxes upon the population. Nonetheless, the picture we have here shows some semblance of mutual respect between the two parties. The Jewish elders say that the centurion "loves our nation and he built the synagogue for us" (v. 5). Furthermore, the centurion exhibits all the signs of faith in the Lord God that the religious Jew shows. It seems that Luke

worthy to have you enter under my roof. ⁷Therefore, I did not consider myself worthy to come to you; but say the word and let my servant be healed. ⁸For I too am a person subject to authority, with soldiers subject to me. And I say to one, 'Go,' and he goes; and to another, 'Come here,' and he comes; and to my slave, 'Do this,' and he does it." ⁹When Jesus heard this he was amazed at him and, turning, said to the crowd following him, "I tell you, not even in Israel have I found such faith." ¹⁰When the messengers returned to the house, they found the slave in good health.

Raising of the Widow's Son. ¹¹Soon ▶ afterward he journeyed to a city called Nain, and his disciples and a large crowd accompanied him. ¹²As he drew near to the gate of the city, a man who

---

has described a "God-fearer," a Gentile who found the monotheistic God of the Jews and their moral code appealing, but who was unable or unwilling to separate himself from his own family and ethnic group by dietary laws or circumcision (see Acts 10:22). Thus the Jewish elders in verse 4 can speak highly of the centurion. In addition, knowing that a religious Jew could not enter a Gentile house, the centurion obviates a potentially embarrassing situation by sending a second band of emissaries, this time "friends," with the advice that Jesus perform his deed from afar. Luke probably included this passage to support the place of Gentiles within the Jewish-Christian movement. As Jesus comes to the Gentile centurion, so, too, does he come to Gentiles in the Mediterranean world.

Finally, we see a positive exchange between the Jewish elders and Jesus. Although Luke often describes a great deal of tension between Pharisaical parties and Jesus, the relationship between Jesus and the Jews is not always hostile, as we see here. The elders may not be Pharisees specifically but may have some position of authority in the community, indicating some degree of formal adherence to the Mosaic Law.

The ruins of the second-century synagogue in Capernaum rest on a foundation of an earlier one, which according to one tradition is the synagogue in question here.

7:11-17 The son of the widow of Nain

This story is found only in Luke, and it is the first occurrence of restoring the dead to life found in this Gospel.

Tradition locates Nain on the southwest side of the Carmel mountain range in Galilee. That the prophet Elisha performed a similar miracle in Shunem, on the northeast side of the same mountain range, no doubt influences the response of the crowd here (see 2 Kgs 4:8-37); they exclaim, "A great prophet has arisen in our midst" (v. 16). Some commentators also

had died was being carried out, the only son of his mother, and she was a widow. A large crowd from the city was with her. [13]When the Lord saw her, he was moved with pity for her and said to her, "Do not weep." [14]He stepped forward and touched the coffin; at this the bearers halted, and he said, "Young man, I tell you, arise!" [15]The dead man sat up and began to speak, and Jesus gave him to his mother. [16]Fear seized them all, and they glorified God, exclaiming, "A great prophet has arisen in our midst," and "God has visited his people." [17]This report about him spread through the whole of Judea and in all the surrounding region.

The Messengers from John the Baptist. [18]The disciples of John told him about all these things. John summoned two of his disciples [19]and sent them to the Lord to ask, "Are you the one who is to come, or should we look for another?" [20]When the men came to him, they said, "John the Baptist has sent us to you to ask, 'Are you the one who is

---

see an allusion to Elijah's raising the son of the widow of Zarephath, near Sidon in present-day Lebanon (1 Kgs 17:8-24).

In both these accounts the respective prophet resuscitates the dead by lying on top of them several times, and this point highlights the difference they have with the story involving Jesus at Nain. Here Jesus simply commands the young man to rise. The action reflects Jesus' authority, and the crowd recognizes this fact.

7:18-23 The messengers from John the Baptist

This passage is the first formal encounter between John the Baptist and Jesus. Though John baptizes Jesus in 3:21-22, he does so unknowingly. The infancy narratives show the accounts dealing with the Baptist preceding those of Jesus; for example, the annunciation to Zechariah and John's birth come before the annunciation to Mary and Jesus' birth in Bethlehem. This pattern emphasizes that John the Baptist is not the Messiah, but the precursor to the Messiah. Such an understanding is underscored at the baptism and is further clarified here. John the Baptist has seen himself as the forerunner (see 3:16-17). In sending disciples to ask such a question of Jesus now, he seeks confirmation that Jesus is the Messiah for whom he has prepared the way.

The Baptist's disciples in this narrative also play a role for the early church. At this time (A.D. 80–90) and even later, there was tension between the followers of John and those of Jesus. Luke's construction of having John's disciples asking Jesus if they "should . . . look for another" (vv. 19-20) serves as the Christian community's invitation to the Baptist's disciples to join the ranks of Jesus' followers.

to come, or should we look for another?'" ²¹At that time he cured many of their diseases, sufferings, and evil spirits; he also granted sight to many who were blind. ²²And he said to them in reply, "Go and tell John what you have seen and heard: the blind regain their sight, the lame walk, lepers are cleansed, the deaf hear, the dead are raised, the poor have the good news proclaimed to them. ²³And blessed is the one who takes no offense at me."

Jesus' Testimony to John. ²⁴When the messengers of John had left, Jesus began to speak to the crowds about John. "What did you go out to the desert to see—a reed swayed by the wind? ²⁵Then what did you go out to see? Someone dressed in fine garments? Those who dress luxuriously and live

Jesus' answer to the Baptist's messengers is based on his ministry thus far, including the raising of the dead, as seen at Nain, which Luke places immediately before this passage. Jesus' response draws on Old Testament prophecy, especially the sayings of the prophet Isaiah (29:18-19; 35:5-6; 61:1), whose preaching is echoed in the synagogue at Nazareth (see Luke 4:18-21). In framing his words by citations from Isaiah, we see how Judaism forms the crucial context for understanding the Gospels and the New Testament.

7:24-35 Jesus and John

Jesus' testimony about John lessens the tensions between their respective disciples as it extends a welcoming embrace to the Baptist's followers. Jesus, the true Messiah, has tremendous regard and respect for John the Baptist: "A prophet? Yes, I tell you, and more than a prophet" (7:26).

The schism motif resurfaces at verses 29-30. Some who had chosen John's baptism see the plan of God fulfilled in Jesus, and others who had rejected John's baptism also reject Jesus and his message. In this latter group, Jesus mentions specifically Pharisees and scholars of the Law. The analogy of the children in the marketplace (vv. 31-32) is apt for them. No matter what the message or the deed, many people will find fault with God's design, because accepting the will of God necessitates a change in one's behavior. It would be wrong to assume that no Pharisees or scribes were disciples either of John or of Jesus; the reign of God split that group as well (see 7:1-10, 36-50; 13:31-33; 14:1-6). The hardness of heart they exhibit here crosses all class divisions.

Lest we tend to overlook the joy Jesus had in his earthly life, it would be good to note that he seems to have had the reputation of relishing good food and drink, as verses 33-34 suggest (see also 5:30; 7:36-50; 10:38-42). In addition, many of his parables and allusions are based on feasting metaphors (see 14:7-14, 15-24). As seen throughout Luke's Gospel, attention to

sumptuously are found in royal pal-
aces. ²⁶Then what did you go out to
see? A prophet? Yes, I tell you, and
more than a prophet. ²⁷This is the one
about whom scripture says:

'Behold, I am sending my messenger ahead of you,
he will prepare your way before
you.'

²⁸I tell you, among those born of
women, no one is greater than John; yet
the least in the kingdom of God is
greater than he." ²⁹(All the people who
listened, including the tax collectors,
and who were baptized with the baptism of John, acknowledged the righteousness of God; ³⁰but the Pharisees
and scholars of the law, who were not
baptized by him, rejected the plan of
God for themselves.)

³¹"Then to what shall I compare the
people of this generation? What are
they like? ³²They are like children who
sit in the marketplace and call to one
another,

'We played the flute for you, but
you did not dance.
We sang a dirge, but you did not
weep.'

³³For John the Baptist came neither eating food nor drinking wine, and you
said, 'He is possessed by a demon.'
³⁴The Son of Man came eating and
drinking and you said, 'Look, he is a
glutton and a drunkard, a friend of tax
collectors and sinners.' ³⁵But wisdom is
vindicated by all her children."

The Pardon of the Sinful Women.
³⁶A Pharisee invited him to dine with
him, and he entered the Pharisee's

---

conversion, concern for the poor, and enjoyment of all God's gifts go hand
in hand. A dour disciple does not further the reign of God.

7:36-50 The woman of loving gratitude

It is often assumed that the woman is guilty of some kind of sexual sin,
yet there is nothing in the text to suggest such a conclusion. The material
concerning John the Baptist ("the poor have the good news proclaimed to
them"—7:22) forms a good context for this passage. In the tradition this
story becomes entangled with Matthew 26:6-13; Mark 14:3-9; John 12:1-8,
all recording the anointing at Bethany on the journey to Jerusalem. In
Luke, Jesus does not turn toward Jerusalem until 9:51, so this occasion, in
the Lukan literary outline at least, is set in Galilee.

Simon the Pharisee's lack of attention to the details of hospitality
notwithstanding, such an incident would be shocking in any case. Guests
would have been reclining around the outside rim of a *triclinium*, a horseshoe-shaped table. While the left side of their torsos rested on elevated
cushions to allow them to take food and drink with their right hand, their
feet would be exposed to the wall's perimeter. Before the second century,
the Roman custom was to have the *triclinium* open or near the *atrium*.

house and reclined at table. ³⁷Now there was a sinful woman in the city who learned that he was at table in the house of the Pharisee. Bringing an alabaster flask of ointment, ³⁸she stood behind him at his feet weeping and began to bathe his feet with her tears. Then she wiped them with her hair, kissed them, and anointed them with the ointment. ³⁹When the Pharisee who had invited him saw this he said to himself, "If this man were a prophet, he would know who and what sort of woman this is who is touching him, that she is a sinner." ⁴⁰Jesus said to him in reply, "Simon, I have something to say to you." "Tell me, teacher," he said.

⁴¹"Two people were in debt to a certain creditor; one owed five hundred days' wages and the other owed fifty. ⁴²Since they were unable to repay the debt, he forgave it for both. Which of them will love him more?" ⁴³Simon said in reply, "The one, I suppose, whose larger debt was forgiven." He said to him, "You have judged rightly." ⁴⁴Then he turned to the woman and said to Simon, "Do you see this woman? When I entered your house, you did not give me water for my feet, but she has bathed them with her tears and wiped them with her hair. ⁴⁵You did not give me a kiss, but she has not ceased kissing my feet since the time I entered. ⁴⁶You did not

Such an arrangement would explain how the woman gained access to the house. Nonetheless, she would have had to crawl around the outside rim of the table until she found the right set of feet before she could start the anointing. Even with the broadest, most accepting, and opened mind and heart, and even within the public culture of the Mideast, her actions would have been seen as suspicious or at least bizarre. Simon's consternation is understandable, if not permissible.

The text does not mention what kind of ointment the woman uses, but if it is contained in an alabaster jar, it would have been very expensive. The juxtaposition of using this ointment on the feet when the guest should have been anointed on the head accentuates the great release of guilt and shame this woman feels from having encountered Jesus somewhere along the way.

Jesus does not defend the woman by saying that she is sinless; rather, he acknowledges her sins and forgives them. The parable forms the interpretation of the event. Everyone is a sinner and everyone needs forgiveness. Only when we realize that we need the grace of Christ, do we see what a great gift the forgiveness is. This woman becomes the model of the proper response of limitless gratitude all people should show in light of the salvation Christ offers.

Simon's inner thoughts (v. 39) have an ironic twist. Jesus *is* a prophet, and he *does* know what kind of woman this is. That is why he responds in such a manner.

anoint my head with oil, but she anointed my feet with ointment. ⁴⁷So I tell you, her many sins have been forgiven; hence, she has shown great love. But the one to whom little is forgiven, loves little." ⁴⁸He said to her, "Your sins are forgiven." ⁴⁹The others at table said to themselves, "Who is this who even forgives sins?" ⁵⁰But he said to the woman, "Your faith has saved you; go in peace."

8 **Galilean Women Follow Jesus.** ¹Afterward he journeyed from one town and village to another, preaching and proclaiming the good news of the kingdom of God. Accompanying him were the Twelve ²and some women who had been cured of evil spirits and infirmities, Mary, called Magdalene, from whom seven demons had gone out, ³Joanna, the wife of Herod's steward Chuza, Susanna, and many others who provided for them out of their resources.

The Parable of the Sower. ⁴When a large crowd gathered, with people from one town after another journeying to him, he spoke in a parable. ⁵"A sower went out to sow his seed. And as

8:1-3 Women disciples from Galilee

Jesus' ministry is sustained and supported by the resources of several wealthy women disciples; three are named here: Mary Magdalene, Joanna, and Susanna. Joanna's marriage to Herod's steward, Chuza, certainly raises speculation on how much Herod and his court would have known about Jesus.

Luke refers to Mary Magdalene as one "from whom seven demons had gone out" (v. 2). The longer ending of Mark is the only other place in the Gospel tradition that describes her similarly (Mark 16:9). Exactly what is meant by the "seven demons" is unclear. If Jesus performed an exorcism over Mary Magdalene, there is no record of it, save for these verses from Luke and Mark; "seven demons" heightens the severity of her earlier possession.

The other evangelists do not name the women disciples until the death account (see Matt 27:56; Mark 15:40; John 19:25). Because he names the women here, Luke, who avoids repetitions, does not identify them at the crucifixion scene. He does name Mary Magdalene and Joanna as witnesses to the resurrection, however (24:10).

This group of men and women will follow Jesus to Jerusalem and remain there through the resurrection, but only the women and some of the men will stand at the cross (23:49).

8:4-18 Parables and response

The parable of the sower and its explanation appear in all three Synoptics. Luke's rendition, as usual, is a more compact version of this familiar

he sowed, some seed fell on the path and was trampled, and the birds of the sky ate it up. ⁶Some seed fell on rocky ground, and when it grew, it withered for lack of moisture. ⁷Some seed fell among thorns, and the thorns grew with it and choked it. ⁸And some seed fell on good soil, and when it grew, it produced fruit a hundredfold." After saying this, he called out, "Whoever has ears to hear ought to hear."

The Purpose of the Parables. ⁹Then his disciples asked him what the meaning of this parable might be. ¹⁰He answered, "Knowledge of the mysteries of the kingdom of God has been granted to you; but to the rest, they are made known through parables so that

---

story, leaving out the detail about the scorching sun, the shallow depth of rocky soil, and the trampled path. While Matthew 13:2 and Mark 4:1 state that the large crowd forces Jesus to preach from a boat, Luke has Jesus standing in the boat earlier in the Gospel narrative (see 5:1-11). Luke also underscores that the people come to him "from one town after another" (v. 4); Jesus' reputation has spread.

In verses 9-10 Jesus offers an explanation for parables. The "mysteries of the kingdom" (v. 10) are most probably the intuitive knowledge that comes with the intimacy the disciples have with Jesus. Paradoxically, Jesus must still explain the parable to them. This explanation can also be a reference to Isaiah 6:9-10: "Listen carefully, but you shall not understand! / Look intently, but you shall know nothing!"

That this parable is one of the clearest makes Jesus' commenting on it a puzzlement. Surely there are more difficult parables than this one that demand explanations. This dialogue, however, is the logical follow-up to the preceding one concerning the purpose of parables and an example of that intimacy the disciples have with the Lord. Its presence in the text most probably reflects the redaction of the early church in trying to underline the qualities of good disciples.

The term "seed" occurs six times in Matthew and Mark and four times in Luke. Most of the instances are in this parable and its explanation in all three Synoptics. Its use here and elsewhere shows that the word "seed" represents either the word of God or faith.

Naturally, among farmers the image is apt, and particularly so for Luke, who is writing for a community that tradition locates in Syria, one of the ancient world's breadbaskets. The farmers at this time would not plant the seed in rows as is done today; rather, they would walk along broadcasting the seed in front of them.

Any interpretation of this parable should allow for the fact that there is no limit given to the number of times the sower casts the seed. Just as a

'they may look but not see, and hear but not understand.'

The Parable of the Sower Explained. [11]"This is the meaning of the parable. The seed is the word of God. [12]Those on the path are the ones who have heard, but the devil comes and takes away the word from their hearts that they may not believe and be saved. [13]Those on rocky ground are the ones who, when they hear, receive the word with joy, but they have no root; they believe only for a time and fall away in time of trial. [14]As for the seed that fell among thorns, they are the ones who have heard, but as they go along, they are choked by the anxieties and riches and pleasures of life, and they fail to produce mature fruit. [15]But as for the seed that fell on rich soil, they are the ones who, when they have heard the word, embrace it with a generous and good heart, and bear fruit through perseverance.

The Parable of the Lamp. [16]"No one who lights a lamp conceals it with a vessel or sets it under a bed; rather, he places it on a lampstand so that those who enter may see the light. [17]For there is nothing hidden that will not become visible, and nothing secret that will not be known and come to light. [18]Take care, then, how you hear. To anyone who has, more will be given, and from the one who has not, even what he seems to have will be taken away."

Jesus and His Family. [19]Then his mother and his brothers came to him

---

sower will go out at least once a year to plant, so will the word continue to fall on the soil. The emphasis in the parable is on the soil and the soil's response, not on the seed or the sower.

The connection that the parable of the lamp has with the explanation of the sower and the seed flows smoothly from Luke's hand. In a mixing of metaphors, the seed that has taken root in good soil now becomes a lamp. The knowledge of the mysteries of the kingdom, which we meet in verse 10, is catalyzed by the interpretation in verse 18: "To anyone who has, more will be given, and from the one who has not, even what he seems to have will be taken away." This verse is not describing the moral order; rather, it expresses growth in the word of God. Love and devotion to God build upon themselves and increase within a person to the point that others are drawn to God and the kingdom by the life of those who have let their seed flourish and their light shine. Jesus reiterates this theme when talking about the mustard seed (see Luke 13:19; 17:6).

8:19-21 Jesus and his family

Luke is less harsh in recording this event than either of the other two synoptic writers. Jesus' mother and brothers are unable to reach him "because of the crowd." In the parallel accounts in Matthew and Mark, his mother and brothers come calling for him as if he were a family embarrassment.

but were unable to join him because of the crowd. [20]He was told, "Your mother and your brothers are standing outside and they wish to see you." [21]He said to them in reply, "My mother and my brothers are those who hear the word of God and act on it."

The Calming of a Storm at Sea. [22]One day he got into a boat with his disciples and said to them, "Let us cross to the other side of the lake." So they set sail, [23]and while they were sailing he fell asleep. A squall blew over the lake, and they were taking in water and were in danger. [24]They came and woke him saying, "Master, master, we are perishing!" He awakened, rebuked the wind and the waves, and they subsided and there was a calm. [25]Then he asked them, "Where is your faith?" But

The question of Jesus' brothers often arises, especially in the Catholic tradition, which holds that Jesus was the only child of Mary. Explanations that the Greek word for "brother," *adelphos,* can also mean "cousin" are not at all convincing. A better basis for the claim is also founded on tradition, which sees Joseph as a man older than the young woman Mary. This tradition holds that Joseph lost his first wife to childbirth, a death common for women throughout history. Jesus' brothers, then, are really Jesus' half-brothers from Joseph's first marriage. It is impossible to prove or disprove the details of Mary's perpetual virginity. Of course, the virginal conception of Jesus is not the issue under discussion here. Luke is explicit, as is Matthew, that when Mary was pregnant with Jesus, no human father was involved (see above, Luke 1:26-38).

This short passage redefines human relationships under Christ. At this time and place, the extended family was one's first and only locus of identification. To lose or be ostracized from the family was equivalent to losing all personhood. Jesus redefines the lines of association and kinship by broadening the family boundary. Now, the evangelist seems to say, disciples form a new family, which is all-inclusive of those who hear and do the word of God. These new bonds of relationship are developed in Luke's second volume, the Acts of the Apostles.

8:22-25 The calming of the storm

With the phrase "One day" Luke shifts from Jesus' preaching to his performing miracles. The Lake of Galilee, below sea level and surrounded by hills and mountains, is well situated for sudden summer storms to arise without warning. As the hot, humid air rises, the colder air comes rushing in, causing large swells in a very small lake. Recent archaeological finds suggest that the boat would most likely have been between eight to nine meters in length (twenty-six to thirty feet), two to three meters wide

they were filled with awe and amazed and said to one another, "Who then is this, who commands even the winds and the sea, and they obey him?"

The Healing of the Gerasene Demoniac. ²⁶Then they sailed to the territory of the Gerasenes, which is opposite Galilee. ²⁷When he came ashore a man from the town who was possessed by demons met him. For a long time he had not worn clothes; he did not live in a house, but lived among the tombs. ²⁸When he saw Jesus, he cried out and fell down before him; in a

---

(seven to nine feet), and about one to two meters high (four to six feet), certainly enough space for Jesus and a large group of disciples.

Although natural phenomena could explain the miracle—these storms subside almost as quickly as they arise— the miraculous lies at the juncture of human experience and divine intervention. People today still speak of a sudden prayer as saving them from a nearly fatal collision. There is no way to prove whether this event of calming the storm occurred or not. The believer would not be wrong to follow the tradition, which says that it did.

The importance of this story, however, is theological. Up until this point, Jesus has been ministering in the Jewish areas on the western and northern shores of the Sea of Galilee. When he says to his disciples, "Let us cross to the other side of the lake" (8:22), he means the eastern shore, which at that time was in the pagan district of the Decapolis, meaning "Ten Cities." Encountering a storm on the lake while heading toward pagan territory shows Jesus in a battle. He is taking on the cosmic forces arrayed against his ministry, and he will not be cowed by them. Here a storm, which in the pagan culture of the surrounding region would have been associated with the god Baal (see 1 Kgs 18), obeys Jesus' command and everyone is saved. He is the Lord of the cosmos.

The story ends with a question, "Who then is this . . ." (v. 25). Luke has been prompting us all along throughout this narrative with questions or statements concerning Jesus' identity (see 4:22, 34, 41; 5:21; 7:16, 49), and the evangelist will continue to do so (see 9:9) before Peter finally declares him to be the Messiah (9:20).

8:26-39 Exorcising the Gerasene demoniac

Having safely crossed the lake, Jesus and the disciples land on the eastern shore, in pagan territory. Immediately demonic forces again challenge Jesus' lordship, but this time from outside the Jewish districts.

All three Synoptics include this account of the Gerasene demoniac. The name of the locale has its textual problems. In the manuscript tradition, an

loud voice he shouted, "What have you to do with me, Jesus, son of the Most High God? I beg you, do not torment me!" [29]For he had ordered the unclean spirit to come out of the man. (It had taken hold of him many times, and he used to be bound with chains and shackles as a restraint, but he would break his bonds and be driven by the demon into deserted places.) [30]Then Jesus asked him, "What is your name?" He replied, "Legion," because many demons had entered him. [31]And they pleaded with him not to order them to depart to the abyss.

[32]A herd of many swine was feeding there on the hillside, and they pleaded with him to allow them to enter those swine; and he let them. [33]The demons came out of the man and entered the swine, and the herd rushed down the steep bank into the lake and was drowned. [34]When the swineherds saw what had happened, they ran away and reported the incident in the town and throughout the countryside. [35]People came out to see what had happened and, when they approached Jesus, they discovered the man from whom the demons had come out sitting at his feet.

---

alternate name for "Gerasene" is "Gadarene," a confusion stemming from the attempts of various scribes to harmonize all three accounts. This attempt at harmonization was further complicated by the fact that Matthew 8:28 reads "Gadarene." The names "Gerasene" and "Gadarene" are based on two separate cities in the Decapolis, Gerasa (or Jerash) and Gadara, respectively. Neither is located on the Sea of Galilee, although Gadara is closer to the lake than Gerasa. Most likely each city's name was used interchangeably as the generic term for the area on the eastern shore, and exacting scribes, trying to address the discrepancies in the text, actually caused more confusion. The tradition locates the site at Kursi, in the northeast quadrant of the Sea of Galilee, which sits on a steep hill above the shoreline.

Not only is the man a demoniac but also, since he lives in tombs, he would be ritually impure to the religious Jews. He calls out to Jesus in a "loud voice" (v. 28), a signal of impending judgment. Unlike Matthew or Mark, Luke notes that Jesus had commanded the spirit to depart from the man even before the demoniac speaks.

Jesus demands the demons' name in order to show his authority over them, although he uses the singular of the noun. To know a name is to exercise control, and the demons freely give it, recognizing that they must be obedient to him. Luke alone states that the demons beg not to be sent to the abyss (v. 31). The swine, impure animals to the Jews, represent the demons' own uncleanness. In biblical Jewish thought, large bodies of water symbolized the entrance to the abyss, or Sheol. In his exorcism, Jesus sends the demons back to where they come from, the dwelling of the

He was clothed and in his right mind, and they were seized with fear. [36]Those who witnessed it told them how the possessed man had been saved. [37]The entire population of the region of the Gerasenes asked Jesus to leave them because they were seized with great fear. So he got into a boat and returned. [38]The man from whom the demons had come out begged to remain with him, but he sent him away, saying, [39]"Return home and recount what God has done for you." The man went off and proclaimed throughout the whole town what Jesus had done for him.

Jairus's Daughter and the Woman with a Hemorrhage. [40]When Jesus returned, the crowd welcomed him, for they were all waiting for him. [41]And a man named Jairus, an official of the synagogue, came forward. He fell at the feet of Jesus and begged him to come to his house, [42]because he had an only daughter, about twelve years old, and she was dying. As he went, the crowds almost crushed him. [43]And a woman afflicted with hemorrhages for twelve years, who [had spent her whole livelihood on doctors and] was unable to be cured by anyone, [44]came up behind him and touched the tassel on his cloak. Immediately her bleeding stopped. [45]Jesus then asked, "Who touched me?" While all were denying it, Peter said, "Master, the crowds are pushing and pressing in upon you." [46]But Jesus said, "Someone ▶

dead. On the one hand, he countermands their wish, and on the other, he proves to all that the demons had actually left the individual.

The pagan man, now free of demons, but bereft of friends and family due to his former state, wants to follow Jesus (v. 38). Jesus turns him into a Gentile missionary going through the city (Gadara? Gerasa?). Thus Luke prepares the reader for the mission to the Gentiles, a major theme in the Acts of the Apostles.

In Luke's narrative of Jesus' earthly ministry, Jesus has been battling the diabolical forces in the world ever since his temptation in the desert. The victory he has with this demoniac functions simultaneously as a realization and as an anticipation of the *eschaton*. In the former, all witness the flight of a legion of evil spirits. Yet the decisive showdown with Satan has yet to occur, and it will not come until Jesus dies and rises in Jerusalem.

8:40-56 Jairus's daughter and the woman with a hemorrhage

Luke follows Mark's order of having one miracle, the hemorrhaging woman, surrounded by another, the raising of Jairus's daughter.

Verse 40 informs us that Jesus has returned to the Jewish districts on the western shore of the Sea of Galilee. Luke, always the evangelist to find joy in the Gospel, specifies that the crowd "welcomed" Jesus. At this point the story of Jairus's daughter is introduced. Verse 42 prepares us for the

has touched me; for I know that power has gone out from me." ⁴⁷When the woman realized that she had not escaped notice, she came forward trembling. Falling down before him, she explained in the presence of all the people why she had touched him and how she had been healed immediately. ⁴⁸He said to her, "Daughter, your faith has saved you; go in peace."

⁴⁹While he was still speaking, someone from the synagogue official's house arrived and said, "Your daughter is dead; do not trouble the teacher any longer." ⁵⁰On hearing this, Jesus answered him, "Do not be afraid; just have faith and she will be saved." ⁵¹When he arrived at the house he allowed no one to enter with him except Peter and John and James, and the child's father and

---

resolution of the story, when the hemorrhaging woman enters the picture in the next verse and turns our attention.

The woman touches the tassel on Jesus' cloak (v. 44). The term "tassel" most likely refers to the fringes religious Jewish men were commanded to wear on the corners of their outer garment in Numbers 15:38. The Greek Old Testament, or Septuagint, calls these tassels *kraspedon*, the same word Luke employs here. The woman is not merely grabbing at Jesus; she wants to clutch the holiest part of his clothing, a sign of her faith. Fearing rebuke, she falls at Jesus' feet. She bears witness to Jesus' miraculous act in front of all (v. 47), while Jesus commends and blesses her. Her faith opened her to Jesus' cure (v. 48).

Luke keeps the narrative flowing by having a messenger arrive from Jairus's house with the news that the young girl is dead (v. 49) even as Jesus is still speaking. When Jesus states that Jairus' daughter is only sleeping, this crowd, different from the one that initially welcomed Jesus, ridicules him. The comparison between the people in the two groups is noteworthy. The first, not enveloped by the fear and dread of losing a child, are in better straits to receive Jesus and his message with happiness and joy. The second, however, watching the passing of the girl and seeing the suffering of the parents, are too preoccupied to concern themselves with Jesus' visit. The Lord's visitation, however, comes to them, too, with the resuscitation of the daughter. Once again, faith is the operative condition for this miracle (v. 50).

Jesus allows only Peter, John, and James to enter the house with him. These three are selected out from the other members of the Twelve at the transfiguration as well (9:28). Peter occupies a central role in the Acts of the Apostles and the early church. John and James are the sons of Zebedee (5:10); the latter was martyred by Herod Agrippa (Acts 12:2), but what of

mother. [52]All were weeping and mourning for her, when he said, "Do not weep any longer, for she is not dead, but sleeping." [53]And they ridiculed him, because they knew that she was dead. [54]But he took her by the hand and called to her, "Child, arise!" [55]Her breath returned and she immediately arose. He then directed that she should be given something to eat. [56]Her parents were astounded, and he instructed them to tell no one what had happened.

9 The Mission of the Twelve. [1]He summoned the Twelve and gave them power and authority over all demons and to cure diseases, [2]and he sent them to proclaim the kingdom of God and to heal [the sick]. [3]He said to them, "Take nothing for the journey, neither walking stick, nor sack, nor food, nor money, and let no one take a second tunic. [4]Whatever house you enter, stay there and leave from there. [5]And as for those who do not welcome you, when you leave that town, shake the dust from your feet in testimony against them." [6]Then they set out and went from village to village proclaiming the good news and curing diseases everywhere.

John? There is a tradition that he is the beloved disciple, the author of the Fourth Gospel (John 13:23; 19:26; 20:2; 21:7, 20-24), but this conclusion cannot be substantiated with absolute certainty. Nonetheless, Paul refers to James, John, and Peter (Kephas) as "pillars" of the church in Jerusalem (Gal 2:9).

9:1-6 The mission of the Twelve

The ninth chapter of Luke introduces a shift in focus. Whereas Luke treats the Galilean ministry in chapters 4 through 8, chapter 9 turns the narrative's attention to the disciples and the beginning of the journey to Jerusalem.

By giving the Twelve authority over the demons, and linking that with the kingdom of God and curing, Luke heightens the eschatological tone of Jesus' ministry. Jesus empowers his followers to join the cosmic battle with Satan. This warfare begins in the temptation scene (Luke 4:1-13) and surfaces throughout the Gospel, coming to a head at the crucifixion.

The injunction to take nothing for the journey ensures complete trust in God. That the Twelve are successful in their curing demonstrates that the kingdom of God has arrived. While this passage is most likely describing the missionary activity of the early church, it does not discount the probability that Jesus had at least the Twelve performing similar deeds in his life on earth. The parallels in the other Synoptics support such an assertion.

The Twelve are commissioned and sent (*apostellō*, 6:2), from which we get the word "apostle." On their names, see Luke 6:12-16.

Herod's Opinion of Jesus. [7]Herod the tetrarch heard about all that was happening, and he was greatly perplexed because some were saying, "John has been raised from the dead"; [8]others were saying, "Elijah has appeared"; still others, "One of the ancient prophets has arisen." [9]But Herod said, "John I beheaded. Who then is this about whom I hear such things?" And he kept trying to see him.

The Return of the Twelve and the Feeding of the Five Thousand. [10]When the apostles returned, they explained to him what they had done. He took them and withdrew in private to a town called Bethsaida. [11]The crowds, meanwhile, learned of this and followed him.

9:7-9 Herod's thoughts

Herod Antipas was tetrarch of Galilee and Perea. His query in verse 9 echoes that of the disciples in the storm-tossed boat in Luke 8:25 and gives the reader an idea of the questions circulating during Christianity's infancy: Who is Jesus, and, in this case, what is his relationship to John the Baptist? In the Jewish tradition, Elijah is supposed to return to usher in the messianic age. See also 23:6-12.

Herod's wily and suspicious nature comes through in this passage. Unlike Matthew and Mark, Luke does not report Herod's infamous birthday celebration, which leads to the beheading of the Baptist, although earlier in his Gospel the third evangelist notifies the reader that Herod has had John imprisoned (3:19-20). From the Jewish historian Josephus, (*Ant.* 18.5.2) we obtain the information that Herod put John to death at his fortress-palace of Machaerus in the Transjordan.

In this description, Josephus also mentions the important detail that Herod feared John because the Baptist drew large crowds. Crowds could always fall into rioting and insurrection. Eventually both Roman and Jewish authorities will have similar fear of Jesus and will form an alliance to execute him as well.

9:10-17 Return of the Twelve and the feeding of the five thousand

Luke, as well as Mark, juxtaposes the return of the apostles with Herod's questioning about Jesus' identity. Herod tries to suppress the movement even as the movement continues to grow despite his efforts. Bethsaida, a town east of the Jordan River but on the northern shore of the Sea of Galilee, is part of the "Gospel Triangle," that segment of the land about which nearly eighty percent of Jesus' ministry takes place. Just south of the town lies a volcanic deposit of basalt rock and rubble making farming or habitation impossible. Most likely this locale is the "private" area mentioned in verse 10.

He received them and spoke to them about the kingdom of God, and he healed those who needed to be cured. ¹²As the day was drawing to a close, the Twelve approached him and said, "Dismiss the crowd so that they can go to the surrounding villages and farms and find lodging and provisions; for we are in a deserted place here." ¹³He said to them, "Give them some food yourselves." They replied, "Five loaves and two fish are all we have, unless we ourselves go and buy food for all these people." ¹⁴Now the men there numbered about five thousand. Then he said to his disciples, "Have them sit down in groups of [about] fifty." ¹⁵They did so and made them all sit down. ¹⁶Then taking the five loaves and the two fish, and looking up to heaven, he said the blessing over them, broke them, and gave them to the disciples to set before the crowd. ¹⁷They all ate and were satisfied. And when the leftover fragments were picked up, they filled twelve wicker baskets.

Peter's Confession about Jesus. ¹⁸Once when Jesus was praying in ▷

The account of the feeding of the five thousand occurs in all four Gospels, though Matthew 15:32-39 and Mark 8:1-10 also feature a feeding of four thousand. The action of first blessing and then breaking the bread has strong eucharistic overtones, and as such, provides eschatological imagery.

Other details play into this imagery as well. Fish, because of their abundance, often symbolize the eschatological banquet. They can also refer to *garum*, a relish made of putrefying fish that was in heavy demand throughout the ancient Mediterranean world. The Greek verb *kataklinō* in verse 14 means to sit or recline at dinner, another reference to the eschatological banquet.

Luke has the crowd gather specifically in groups of fifty, which divides into five thousand evenly. Such a refinement allows Pentecost to function as an interpretive backdrop. In the Jewish tradition at this time, Pentecost was a celebration of the grain harvest and took place fifty days or seven weeks after Passover. In time the feast came to celebrate the giving of the Law to Moses, but whether it commemorated the Sinai covenant at this period is difficult to determine. In any case, the abundance of grain at harvest time symbolizes the abundant blessing of the end times. That five loaves of bread plus two fish equal the number seven underscores the emphasis on Pentecost. Of course, Luke writes about Pentecost in Acts 2, and that feast has prime importance in his work. The feeding of the five thousand, therefore, is one of Luke's ways to foreshadow the *eschaton*.

9:18-27 Peter's confession and the cost of discipleship

Luke is the only evangelist to open the Peter's confession scene with Jesus at prayer. Although Matthew has the most elaborate version of

solitude, and the disciples were with him, he asked them, "Who do the crowds say that I am?" [19]They said in reply, "John the Baptist; others, Elijah; still others, 'One of the ancient prophets has arisen.'" [20]Then he said to them, "But who do you say that I am?" Peter said in reply, "The Messiah of God." [21]He rebuked them and directed them not to tell this to anyone.

The First Prediction of the Passion. [22]He said, "The Son of Man must suffer greatly and be rejected by the elders, the chief priests, and the scribes, and be killed and on the third day be raised."

The Conditions of Discipleship. [23]Then he said to all, "If anyone wishes to come after me, he must deny himself and take up his cross daily and follow me. [24]For whoever wishes to save his life will lose it, but whoever loses his life for my sake will save it. [25]What profit is there for one to gain the whole world yet lose or forfeit himself? [26]Whoever is ashamed of me and of my words, the Son of Man will be ashamed of when he comes in his glory and in the glory of the Father and of the holy angels. [27]Truly I say to you, there are some standing here who will

Peter's confession, the other synoptic writers recount it. In all three Gospels, Jesus poses the question to the disciples, but Peter is the only one who answers. Their comments about John the Baptist and Elijah recapitulate Herod's thoughts in trying to identify Jesus. Elijah was the prophet whose return would usher in the coming of the Messiah. John the Baptist, as precursor, fits into this category as well, and mention of his name here reflects the early Christian community's appeal to the Baptist's disciples, who still feel that the Baptist is the Messiah.

All Synoptics display a set of three passion predictions. This one is Luke's first (see 9:44; 18:31-33). The context colors the moment. The eschatological overtones in both the feeding of the five thousand and Peter's confession take on a stark reality in the passion prediction. Yes, Jesus is the Messiah ushering in a new age in which all can participate, but that new age comes with a price.

An aphorism encapsulates one of the great paradoxes of Christian life: gain is really loss and loss is really gain (v. 24). In the Lukan narrative, these words prepare the disciples for what lies ahead as it encourages the Lukan community. The eschatological term "Son of Man," along with one of Luke's favorite phrases, "kingdom of God," reaffirms the eschatological dimension that must be a part of any disciple of Christ.

9:28-36 The transfiguration of Jesus

Chapter 9 continues to focus on the small group of disciples, and once again we see Jesus at prayer. The interplay between the mission, eschato-

not taste death until they see the kingdom of God."

The Transfiguration of Jesus. [28]About eight days after he said this, he took Peter, John, and James and went up the mountain to pray. [29]While he was praying his face changed in appearance and his clothing became dazzling white. [30]And behold, two men were conversing with him, Moses and Elijah, [31]who appeared in glory and spoke of his exodus that he was going to accomplish in Jerusalem. [32]Peter and his companions had been overcome by sleep, but becoming fully awake, they saw his glory and the two men standing with him. [33]As they were about to part from him, Peter said to Jesus, "Master, it is good that we are here; let us make three tents, one for you, one for Moses, and one for

logical feeding, confession, passion prediction, conditions of discipleship, and now transfiguration form a synthesis of Christian life.

What is the purpose of following Jesus, and where will it all lead? Luke as well as Matthew and Mark answers the question with the transfiguration. Many consider this event to be an account of a post-resurrection appearance. That all three Synoptics situate it within the ministry, however, militates against such an interpretation. It is better to view it as a foreshadowing of the glorification of the resurrection. Placed within this context of passion predictions and discipleship, the transfigured Christ shows the disciples, through Peter, James, and John, the promise that discipleship can bring both to this life and the life to come.

Moses and Elijah, representing the Law and the Prophets, respectively, give their approbation to what the disciples are seeing. Elijah's presence also has an element of foreshadowing; according to Jewish tradition, he is to usher in the messianic age. Both these worthies speak to Jesus of the "exodus" he is about to accomplish in Jerusalem (v. 31). "Exodus" has a double meaning. Naturally, the reader draws on the account of the Israelites' deliverance from death and slavery in Egypt to freedom and new life in the Promised Land. "Exodus," however, can also refer to death. On this basis, Jesus' death is a deliverance from slavery to new life, and his exodus is completed at the resurrection and ascension. Because so much of the material in this chapter deals with discipleship, the meaning death has for Jesus is the same for those who follow him.

The voice from the cloud resonates with the voice at the baptism (3:21-22), but with two differences. At the baptism, Luke writes, the voice comes from heaven and says, "You are my beloved Son; with you I am well pleased"; but here at the transfiguration, the voice comes from the cloud and says, "This is my chosen Son, listen to him" (v. 35). Because the

Elijah." But he did not know what he was saying. ³⁴While he was still speaking, a cloud came and cast a shadow over them, and they became frightened when they entered the cloud. ³⁵Then from the cloud came a voice that said, "This is my chosen Son; listen to him." ³⁶After the voice had spoken, Jesus was found alone. They fell silent and did not at that time tell anyone what they had seen.

The Healing of a Boy with a Demon. ³⁷On the next day, when they came down from the mountain, a large crowd met him. ³⁸There was a man in the crowd who cried out, "Teacher, I beg you, look at my son; he is my only child. ³⁹For a spirit seizes him and he suddenly screams and it convulses him until he foams at the mouth; it releases him only with difficulty, wearing him out. ⁴⁰I begged your disciples to cast it

---

voice from heaven at the baptism is in the second person, only Jesus hears it. At the transfiguration, the voice is in the third person, allowing the three disciples to hear it as well. The reference to the cloud is an echo from Exodus, where the glory of God's presence (Shekinah) is depicted as a cloud (Exod 13:21). God is present at the transfiguration too.

In Matthew's and Mark's version of the transfiguration, Jesus commands the three disciples not to say anything about what they had seen. Luke simply writes, however, that the three kept silent about the whole event "at that time" (v. 36). Although noting that the place of the transfiguration was of no importance to Luke, the tradition, based on Matthew 17:1 and Mark 9:2, locates it on Mount Tabor.

Placed in the context of the mission, eschatology, passion, and discipleship, the transfiguration becomes part of the promise to those who follow Jesus. As he is transfigured into glory by following the Father's will, so too will each Christian disciple be transfigured.

9:37-50 Exorcism and lessons on the kingdom

This case of demonic possession balances the eschatological tone of transfigured glorification by interjecting an attack from the realm of evil. Though the boy's symptoms seem like a case of epilepsy, and may very well have been, sickness was often attributed to the machinations of the devil. In the sense that goodness is from God and illness is not a good, the ancient interpretation hits the mark. Jesus, the one whom Peter confesses as the Messiah and the one whose glory is seen in the transfiguration, reclaims creation for God in the cure of the possessed boy. Only Luke concludes this story by saying that all were "astonished by the majesty of God" (v. 43). Not only does this bit of editing direct attention to the true source and goal of the exorcism, but it also enables the evangelist to omit

out but they could not." [41]Jesus said in reply, "O faithless and perverse generation, how long will I be with you and endure you? Bring your son here." [42]As he was coming forward, the demon threw him to the ground in a convulsion; but Jesus rebuked the unclean spirit, healed the boy, and returned him to his father. [43]And all were astonished by the majesty of God.

The Second Prediction of the Passion. While they were all amazed at his every deed, he said to his disciples, [44]"Pay attention to what I am telling you. The Son of Man is to be handed over to men." [45]But they did not understand this saying; its meaning was hidden from them so that they should not understand it, and they were afraid to ask him about this saying.

The Greatest in the Kingdom. [46]An argument arose among the disciples about which of them was the greatest. [47]Jesus realized the intention of their hearts and took a child and placed it by his side [48]and said to them, "Whoever receives this child in my name receives me, and whoever receives me receives

---

verses that underscore the disciples' poor performance (see Matt 17:19-20; Mark 9:28-29). In his harsh words, Jesus shows his frustration in getting the message across to those closest to him (v. 41).

While all are marveling at God's greatness, Jesus predicts his passion for the second time (vv. 45-46). The redemption of creation will not be easy and will not be without suffering and death, a sober reminder after the transfiguration and the exorcism. The Lukan Jesus is emphatic about the suffering he must undergo (v. 44). Matthew and Mark do not include this heightened urgency in their parallel accounts. All three Synoptics, however, show the disciples afraid to ask for clarification about the upcoming passion. Luke states that the meaning was "hidden" from them (v. 45), a comment that ties into Jesus' frustration at verse 41 and leads into the instruction on greatness.

The disciples have difficulty comprehending the meaning behind the life and work of Jesus, as the argument about greatness demonstrates (vv. 46-48). With all they have seen in the ministry, all they have experienced by way of miracles, healings, and for at least three of them, the transfiguration, they still measure success according to the world's standards. The child whom Jesus placed at his side was most probably part of a group of children who would beg, pester, and tag along with these strangers for part of the distance through a town. Receiving a child like this is not always easy to do, yet that is the point of Jesus' action. Furthermore, in the society of that time, children were obligated to show respect to adults, not vice versa. The placement of this pericope after the second passion prediction for a lesson on greatness is particularly apropos.

the one who sent me. For the one who is least among all of you is the one who is the greatest."

Another Exorcist. [49]Then John said in reply, "Master, we saw someone casting out demons in your name and we tried to prevent him because he does not follow in our company." [50]Jesus said to him, "Do not prevent him, for whoever is not against you is for you."

V. The Journey to Jerusalem: Luke's Travel Narrative

Departure for Jerusalem; Samaritan Inhospitality. [51]When the days for his being taken up were fulfilled, he resolutely determined to journey to Jerusalem, [52]and he sent messengers ahead of him. On the way they entered a Samaritan village to prepare for his reception there, [53]but they would not welcome

---

The account about another exorcist (vv. 49-50) highlights the dispute about prestige and the rivalry the disciples have among themselves. The jealousies of the petty despots who ruled all of Palestine often prevented them from working toward mutual self-interest. For the Christian, the horizon line must be higher.

THE JOURNEY TO JERUSALEM

Luke 9:51–19:27

In all three Synoptic accounts, Jesus makes only one trip to Jerusalem, and that journey ends in his passion, death, and resurrection. Luke is the only evangelist, however, to magnify Jerusalem's theological purpose; it is the crucible into which Jesus' whole earthly ministry is funneled. Jerusalem becomes the city of destiny.

This point also marks the beginning of what some scholars call the "Big Interpolation," a large section of material that cannot be linked to Mark and, with few exceptions, has no parallel in Q. The interpolation extends to 18:14.

9:51-56 Departure for Jerusalem and Samaritan inhospitality

Luke describes the shift toward the holy city most dramatically (v. 51). The phrase "When the days for being taken up were fulfilled" signals the end of his Galilean ministry according to a divine plan. "He resolutely determined to journey to Jerusalem" shows an intensity of purpose in completing that divine plan. Luke's vocabulary in verse 51 breathes with metaphor. The Greek for "being taken up, received up" is the word *analēmpsis,* which means both "ascension" and "death." When combined with the "exodus" referred to in the transfiguration (v. 31), there develops the composite picture of death and glorification.

him because the destination of his journey was Jerusalem. ⁵⁴When the disciples James and John saw this they asked, "Lord, do you want us to call down fire from heaven to consume them?" ⁵⁵Jesus turned and rebuked them, ⁵⁶and they journeyed to another village.

The Would-be Followers of Jesus. ⁵⁷As they were proceeding on their journey someone said to him, "I will follow you wherever you go." ⁵⁸Jesus answered him, "Foxes have dens and birds of the sky have nests, but the Son of Man has nowhere to rest his head." ⁵⁹And to another he said, "Follow me." But he replied, "[Lord,] let me go first and bury my father." ⁶⁰But he answered him, "Let the dead bury their dead. But you, go

Jesus is going up, both literally and figuratively. Jerusalem is over 900 meters (2700 feet) above sea level, while the Sea of Galilee is nearly 100 meters (300 feet) below; he and his disciples must climb the Judean mountains to reach the city. Metaphorically, after the passion, death, and resurrection, Jesus will ascend to the Father, an ascension that also is his glorification. These events begin and, in a large way, take place within the time frame of Passover, the Jewish commemoration of the Exodus.

Luke's detail about passing through the Samaritan villages raises some questions. Jews in Galilee would avoid passing through Samaria as they made their way south to Jerusalem. The usual route was to walk along the Jordan Valley and begin the ascent at Jericho. It appears that Luke might be relying on some ancient tradition that Jesus passed through, if not ministered in, Samaria. John's story of the Samaritan woman at the well (4:4-41) corroborates Jesus' presence in that territory. Moreover, according to Acts, Samaria was the first non-Jewish region to be converted to Christianity. This short foray into Samaria functions as a foreshadowing of the missionary activity that the Acts of the Apostles will detail. Jesus' rebuke constitutes his stand against vengeance and violence, as well as reflecting his attitude toward missionary activity (see 9:5).

9:57-62 Would-be followers of Jesus

Whereas the disciples have already heard the discourse on the cost of discipleship (see 9:23-27), others joining Jesus have not. Jesus relates the proper comportment in three situations: one to a person who is ready to give all for the kingdom, another to a person who is asked to give all for the kingdom, and still another to one who wants to hold back from giving all to the kingdom. Jesus challenges them by using imagery and hyperbole. The curt answers he gives show the rhythm of someone hurrying with a direct purpose in mind, and the vacillation Jesus encounters with these three would deflect from that purpose.

View of Jerusalem from a Jewish cemetery below the Mount of Olives

and proclaim the kingdom of God." [61]And another said, "I will follow you, Lord, but first let me say farewell to my family at home." [62][To him] Jesus said, "No one who sets a hand to the plow and looks to what was left behind is fit for the kingdom of God."

10 The Mission of the Seventy-two. [1]After this the Lord appointed seventy [-two] others whom he sent ahead of him in pairs to every town and place he intended to visit. [2]He said to them, "The harvest is abundant but the laborers are few; so ask the master of the harvest to send out laborers for his harvest. [3]Go on your way; behold, I am sending you like lambs among wolves. [4]Carry no money bag, no sack, no sandals; and greet no one along the way. [5]Into whatever house

To the first individual, Jesus underscores that personal comfort will often have to give way to the demands of discipleship. His response to the second may seem harsh, but in no way is it to be understood as negating one's obligations to one's parents or family. Rather, Jesus is seeing through what constitutes a lame excuse while speaking on a symbolic level. To follow Jesus is to enter into a life-giving relationship. There are plenty of people who refuse this relationship, and in this sense they are dead; they can bury the physically dead. The reply to the third individual likewise shows the immediacy of the call. In the Jewish and Hellenistic societies, family bonds were very tight and could hold one back from being a disciple. Jesus first addresses this situation in 8:19-21, and his answer here is similar.

10:1-16 The mission of the seventy-two

The ancient manuscripts are evenly divided over whether the mission involves seventy or seventy-two disciples. Both numbers have a basis in the Old Testament. Seventy-two is a multiple of twelve, the number of the tribes of Israel; thus, by their going forth, a like number of disciples could represent the universalism of Jesus' mission. Alternatively, the narrative in Exodus 24 includes seventy elders who ascend the mountain with Moses, thereby making the disciples representatives of the Mosaic tradition.

Luke is the only evangelist to have a commissioning of a second group. In comparing the directives to the seventy-two disciples with the commissioning of the Twelve (9:1-6), we can see some differences as well as some points of contact. The Twelve are given authority over demons and the ability to cure diseases. Furthermore, they are charged with proclaiming the good news. The seventy-two disciples, on the other hand,

you enter, first say, 'Peace to this household.' ⁶If a peaceful person lives there, your peace will rest on him; but if not, it will return to you. ⁷Stay in the same house and eat and drink what is offered to you, for the laborer deserves his payment. Do not move about from one house to another. ⁸Whatever town you enter and they welcome you, eat what is set before you, ⁹cure the sick in it and say to them, 'The kingdom of God is at hand for you.' ¹⁰Whatever town you enter and they do not receive you, go out into the streets and say, ¹¹'The dust of your town that clings to our feet, even that we shake off against you.' Yet know this: the kingdom of God is at hand. ¹²I tell you, it will be more tolerable for Sodom on that day than for that town.

Reproaches to Unrepentant Towns. ¹³"Woe to you, Chorazin! Woe to you, Bethsaida! For if the mighty deeds done in your midst had been done in Tyre and Sidon, they would long ago have repented, sitting in sackcloth and ashes. ¹⁴But it will be more tolerable for Tyre and Sidon at the judgment than for you. ¹⁵And as for you, Capernaum, 'Will you be exalted to heaven? You will go down to the netherworld.'" ¹⁶Whoever listens to you listens to me. Whoever rejects you rejects me. And whoever rejects me rejects the one who sent me."

---

travel in pairs as they bring the good news to households and towns. They are told to cure the sick, but Jesus says nothing about exorcizing demons; yet, they also do so (see v. 17).

Both the Twelve and the seventy-two are to travel light and perform with a singularity of purpose. In this section Jesus calls attention to attributes of Middle Eastern hospitality: there will always be someone to invite them into his or her home. The seventy-two are also told not to abuse the hospitality shown them (v. 8). Both groups are to shake the dust from the street of those towns that do not accept them (v. 11). An important difference, however, is that the seventy-two are to go ahead of Jesus and prepare towns for Jesus' eventual visit.

There is much debate on who constitutes the seventy-two. Were the Twelve selected from the seventy-two, or did they stand independent of them? Were there only seventy-two disciples, or were these seventy-two chosen from a much larger group? Were women in the line of Deborah, Hulda, Esther, Miriam, and Ruth involved, or was the mission restricted to men? These questions are difficult to answer. The important point is that Jesus commissions others to do his work on earth, and as such, the church does that work in him and in his name. Indeed, like the seventy-two, the church prepares the world for Jesus' visitation.

Jesus' comment about Sodom places the Christian message in context. To refuse the redemption he offers is a more heinous sin than any

Return of the Seventy-two. ¹⁷The seventy [-two] returned rejoicing, and said, "Lord, even the demons are subject to us because of your name." ¹⁸Jesus said, "I have observed Satan fall like lightning from the sky. ¹⁹Behold, I have given you the power 'to tread upon serpents' and scorpions and upon the full force of the enemy and nothing will harm you. ²⁰Nevertheless, do not rejoice because the spirits are subject to you, but rejoice because your names are written in heaven."

Praise of the Father. ²¹At that very moment he rejoiced [in] the holy Spirit and said, "I give you praise, Father, Lord of heaven and earth, for although you have hidden these things from the wise and the learned you have revealed them to the childlike. Yes, Father, such has been your gracious will. ²²All things have been handed over to me by my Father. No one knows who the Son is except the Father, and who the Father is except the Son and anyone to whom the Son wishes to reveal him."

transgressions of sexual morality or proper hospitality. Even the Gentile cities of Tyre and Sidon will fare better, since they can read the signs of the times (v. 13).

10:17-20 Return of the seventy-two

The joy of the seventy-two disciples arises from the power they have over demons, a power given them by Jesus and only in his name. Jesus' response in verse 18 seems awkward to many. Some scholars have suggested that the proper translation should be "They have observed Satan fall like lightning from the sky," with the subject of the imperfect verb, *theōreō* ("observe"), being "demons" in verse 17. Greek grammar can support such a construction. A conclusion can be that since the demons see Satan fall from the sky, they easily submit to the disciples. The disciples, empowered by Jesus, become agents with him in furthering the realm of God.

The section closes with Jesus reaffirming the purpose and direction of the disciples' new power. They are not self-serving magicians or sorcerers; they are participants in Jesus' ministry. The disciples, like Jesus and those whom they help, find their reward in God, a point that gains in importance as they follow him to the cross in Jerusalem.

10:21-24 The prayer of Jesus and blessing of the disciples

Luke frequently shows Jesus at prayer. Reflecting the joy the disciples display in their return, Jesus offers praise and thanksgiving to the Father. Luke connects this joy to the Spirit, who, in the Acts of the Apostles, takes on a greater role of consoling and fructifying (see Acts 2:1-36). Luke's re-

The Privileges of Discipleship. ²³Turning to the disciples in private he said, "Blessed are the eyes that see what you see. ²⁴For I say to you, many prophets and kings desired to see what you see, but did not see it, and to hear what you hear, but did not hear it."

The Greatest Commandment. ²⁵There was a scholar of the law who stood up to test him and said, "Teacher, what must I do to inherit eternal life?" ²⁶Jesus said to him, "What is written in the law? How do you read it?" ²⁷He said in reply, "You shall love the Lord, your God, with all your heart, with all your being, with all your strength, and with all your mind, and your neighbor as yourself." ²⁸He replied to him, "You have answered correctly; do this and you will live."

versal theme is evident in verse 21, with revelation coming to the childlike but not to the wise and learned. The whole monologue appears to come from Q (see Matt 11:25-27; 13:16-17) and is one of the few places in the synoptic tradition that shows Jesus explaining his relationship to the Father in a pattern that seems very Johannine.

The disciples, who went out on the mission without money bag, sack, or sandals, receive a great reward in their experience of life in the Lord. The prophets and kings did not see or hear the Messiah of God (Luke 9:20), but the disciples have seen and heard not only the Messiah but also the works done in his name. These works consist in redeeming the world from Satan's clutches.

10:25-29 The greatest commandment

Jesus answers the "scholar of the law" or lawyer with a question. This tack precludes any trap or misunderstanding by unveiling the true motivation on the lawyer's part. The verb "test" in verse 25 is also applied to the devil in the temptation scene (Luke 4:12), thereby emphasizing the sinister quality of the lawyer's question.

Jesus turns the encounter to his advantage. The law that the lawyer quotes is the Jewish Shema, the prayer a devout Jew would recite everyday (Deut 6:4-5). The second half is found in Leviticus 19:18. By endorsing the lawyer's reply, Jesus proves to him and to all listeners that he and his message are not contrary to the Jewish tradition; rather, Jesus forces the audience to see his teaching as an elaboration or refinement of that tradition.

The scholar of the law, however, presses the point with his next question: "And who is my neighbor?" (v. 29). In this verse Luke states that the lawyer wishes to "justify himself," that is, to prove to Jesus in front of the people that he, the legal scholar, is in good stead in the eyes of God. Jesus

The Parable of the Good Samaritan. ²⁹But because he wished to justify himself, he said to Jesus, "And who is my neighbor?" ³⁰Jesus replied, "A man fell victim to robbers as he went down from Jerusalem to Jericho. They stripped and beat him and went off leaving him half-dead. ³¹A priest happened to be going down that road, but when he saw him, he passed by on the opposite side. ³²Likewise a Levite came to the place, and when he saw him, he passed by on the opposite side. ³³But a Samaritan traveler who came upon him was moved with compassion at the sight. ³⁴He approached the victim, poured oil and wine over his wounds and bandaged them. Then he lifted him up on his own animal, took him to an inn and cared for him. ³⁵The next day he took out two silver coins

challenges the lawyer further by responding with the parable of the Good Samaritan.

10:30-37 The parable of the Good Samaritan

Upon the death of King Solomon, Samaria, the region north of Judea, became the center of the northern kingdom at the division of the united monarchy. The Assyrians conquered it in 722 B.C., carted away most of the Israelite inhabitants, and replaced them with conquered peoples from other parts of their empire. These newcomers married into those Israelites left behind, resulting in a population too mixed for the religious Jews in the south to consider part of the covenant. In addition, these northerners, holding only to the books of Genesis through Deuteronomy, maintained their religious cult on Mount Gerizim in Shechem, whereas the Jews in the south saw true worship as taking place only in Jerusalem. The animosity was mutual, as we see in Luke 9:52-54. Samaritans still live and worship on Mount Gerizim today.

This parable exists only in Luke and reflects the theological direction set out in the Gospel and the Acts of the Apostles. The shock value of using a Samaritan as the protagonist in this parable is twofold. The road from Jerusalem to Jericho is solidly in Judea; thus the Samaritan is an unwelcome foreigner in an unfriendly country. The mention of this road also forces the audience to consider the possibility that he has worshiped in Jerusalem. Secondly, for any Samaritans who might hear this parable, this protagonist, by virtue of his journey to Jerusalem, would be a national traitor. On all fronts, then, he can claim no ethnic allegiance, and no people will claim him.

First the priest and then the Levite happen upon the half-dead victim. As officials in the Jerusalem temple, from which they are most probably

and gave them to the innkeeper with the instruction, 'Take care of him. If you spend more than what I have given you, I shall repay you on my way back.' ³⁶Which of these three, in your opinion, was neighbor to the robbers' victim?" ³⁷He answered, "The one who treated him with mercy." Jesus said to him, "Go and do likewise."

Martha and Mary. ³⁸As they continued their journey he entered a village where a woman whose name was Martha welcomed him. ³⁹She had a sister named Mary [who] sat beside the Lord at his feet listening to him speak. ⁴⁰Martha, burdened with much serving, came to him and said, "Lord, do you not care that my sister has left me by

returning, their prime concern is maintaining ritual purity. There has been shedding of blood, and if the man is dead, they would disqualify themselves from any temple service until undergoing the proper ritual purification, a time-consuming practice. They both avoid the problem by crossing to the other side of the road. The only one to respond mercifully is the outsider of two closed societies.

The searing lesson of this parable comes in verses 36-37. The lawyer would know from Leviticus 19:18 that a neighbor is defined as one's countryman and is limited by ethnic background. The parable, however, breaks through such an interpretation. The neighbor is the one who acts compassionately toward another, ethnic divisions notwithstanding.

Although the parable is prompted by an antagonistic question from a Jewish scholar, it would be wrong to think that this parable is addressed only to the ancient Jewish audience. In the Acts of the Apostles, Luke has an evangelizing mission to Samaria. This parable would have been as difficult for Samaritans to listen to as it would have been for the Jews. After all, the Samaritan is in Jewish territory returning from a Jewish holy city, and, depending on how one would want to view the tale, he aids a Jewish unfortunate.

The lesson for the Lukan community is the same for today's reader. To be a neighbor forces a Christian to go beyond friend and family and extend welcome and mercy to the outcast and even to one's enemy.

10:38-42 The discipleship of Martha and Mary

Traditionally, many have seen this story, which appears only in Luke, as a comparison between the Christian active life, symbolized by Martha, and the contemplative life, represented by Mary. Some exegetes interpret it as Luke's subtle way of silencing and sidelining women in the Christian ministry. The Lukan context, as others have pointed out, challenges both these assumptions.

myself to do the serving? Tell her to help me." ⁴¹The Lord said to her in reply, "Martha, Martha, you are anxious and worried about many things. ⁴²There is need of only one thing. Mary has chosen the better part and it will not be taken from her."

11 **The Lord's Prayer.** ¹He was praying in a certain place, and when he had finished, one of his disciples said to him, "Lord, teach us to pray just as John taught his disciples." ²He said to them, "When you pray, say: ▸

> Father, hallowed be your name,
> your kingdom come.
> ³Give us each day our daily bread
> ⁴and forgive us our sins ▸
> for we ourselves forgive everyone in debt to us,
> and do not subject us to the final test."

Mary and Martha share a common ministry in the church. They are models for both men and women of a partnership in service to the reign of God. In this service the love of God is the source and end of all human endeavor, which Mary remembers but Martha seems to have forgotten. The gentle correction that Jesus offers Martha is a reminder to her that work is nothing without its connection to God. For this reason Martha needs Mary as much as Mary needs Martha.

11:1-13 Teachings on prayer

The Our Father or Lord's Prayer (11:1-4) has a revered place within the Christian tradition. With its references to the "name" (v. 2), "bread" (v. 3), and "sins" (v. 4), this prayer underscores a Jewish background. The differences between the Matthean and the Lukan accounts reflect a different theological nuance. While Luke, for example, does not highlight the separation between heaven and earth, Matthew does so by use of such phrases as "Our Father in heaven" (6:9) and "your will be done, / on earth as in heaven" (6:10). This discrepancy led many ancient scribes to try to harmonize Luke's address with Matthew's by adding the phrase "Our . . . in heaven" to "Father" in their versions of Luke's text. Luke's address here, however, matches all the other instances where the Lukan Jesus prays: "I give you praise, Father, Lord of heaven and earth" (10:21); "Father, if you are willing, take this cup away from me" (22:42); "Father, forgive them, they know not what they do" (23:34); and "Father, into your hands I commend my spirit" (23:46).

The structure is the same in the Lukan and Matthean accounts, subtle differences between the two notwithstanding. They both open by hallowing God's name, thereby affirming the divine majesty. They then move to Christ's intermediary role and conclude with a human petition.

Further Teachings on Prayer. ⁵And he said to them, "Suppose one of you has a friend to whom he goes at midnight and says, 'Friend, lend me three loaves of bread, ⁶for a friend of mine has arrived at my house from a journey and I have nothing to offer him,' ⁷and he says in reply from within, 'Do not bother me; the door has already been locked and my children and I are already in bed. I cannot get up to give you anything.' ⁸I tell you, if he does not get up to give him the loaves because of their friendship, he will get up to give him whatever he needs because of his persistence.

The Answer to Prayer. ⁹"And I tell you, ask and you will receive; seek and you will find; knock and the door will be opened to you. ¹⁰For everyone who asks,

---

Many see Luke's use of "sins" as his way of demonstrating Christ's efficacy. With his merciful forgiveness manifested in his passion, death, and resurrection, Jesus defeats Satan by breaking the vicious circle of suffering, fear, hate, and revenge the devil uses to hold humankind in thrall. The person at prayer asks Christ to forgive, and Christ has done so; therefore the person must also forgive.

Matthew's version of the Our Father (see Matt 6:9-13) is better known; indeed, this title for the prayer comes from the Matthew's account and not from Luke's. It is Matthew's rendition that also appears to be the basis for the Our Father found in the early Christian work called the *Didache* (8:2). The *Didache*'s version of the prayer became the form used throughout the centuries and includes the doxology that many Christian churches use in their worship. With the Lord's Prayer as a background, Luke continues the teaching on prayer with the parable of the importunate friend, a reading found only in Luke. Luke's wry comparison between divine response and human reaction— "if he does not get up to give him the loaves because of their friendship, he will get up to give him whatever he needs because of his persistence"—is echoed in the Lukan parable of the persistent widow (18:1-8). The point is that if humans will act on behalf of the petitioner solely from self-serving interest, how much more will God act from love. According to the Palestinian-Jewish custom of the day, the whole family slept on floor bedding in a single room, above the animals. To open the door would not only rouse the family but would also cause a fuss with the livestock, and all in the dark.

Luke tells us how prayers are answered (11:9-13). In his schema they have a natural, thematic, and visual flow from the parable. Someone coming at night would have to *seek* the house and door of a friend. Once found, he or she would have to *knock* at the door persistently to rouse the

receives; and the one who seeks, finds; and to the one who knocks, the door will be opened. ¹¹What father among you would hand his son a snake when he asks for a fish? ¹²Or hand him a scorpion when he asks for an egg? ¹³If you then, who are wicked, know how to give good gifts to your children, how much more will the Father in heaven give the holy Spirit to those who ask him?"

Jesus and Beelzebul. ¹⁴He was driving out a demon [that was] mute, and when the demon had gone out, the mute person spoke and the crowds were amazed. ¹⁵Some of them said, "By the power of Beelzebul, the prince of demons, he drives out demons." ¹⁶Others, to test him, asked him for a sign from heaven. ¹⁷But he knew their thoughts and said to them, "Every kingdom divided against itself will be laid waste and house will fall against house. ¹⁸And if Satan is divided against himself, how will his kingdom stand? For you say that it is by Beelzebul that I drive out demons. ¹⁹If I, then, drive out demons by Beelzebul, by whom do your own people drive them out? Therefore they will be your judges. ²⁰But if it is by the finger of God that [I] drive out demons, then the kingdom of God has come upon you. ²¹When a strong man fully armed guards his palace, his possessions are safe. ²²But when one stronger than he attacks and overcomes him, he takes away the armor on which he relied and dis-

---

inhabitant to *open* it. The references to a snake and a scorpion provide insight into human response to an answered prayer. The listener or hearer would answer the rhetorical questions in verses 11-12 with a firm "None!" Such imagery, however, calls a person to faith. What might appear to be a snake or a scorpion at first glance might actually be the granted request. Again, the reader encounters Luke's analogical style based on divine response and human reaction (11:13).

11:14-23 The Beelzebul controversy

Each Gospel shows some version of the Beelzebul controversy. Although much of this section is from Q, there is evidence of what is called a "Marcan-Q Overlap"; that is, Q material is intricately tied up with Marcan narrative. A comparison between Matthew 12:29, Luke 11:20-21, and Mark 3:27 is such an example. To be sure, there are no Johannine parallels to the synoptic readings here, but there are certainly traces of such accusations against Jesus at several points in the Fourth Gospel: John 7:20; 8:48-52; 10:20-21. This multiple attestation makes certain the conclusion that Jesus was accused of being in league with the devil during his ministry.

Luke uses this pericope as one of the defining moments in his two-volume narrative. Whereas Matthew and Mark both state that someone

tributes the spoils. [23]Whoever is not with me is against me, and whoever does not gather with me scatters.

The Return of the Unclean Spirit. [24]"When an unclean spirit goes out of someone, it roams through arid regions searching for rest but, finding none, it says, 'I shall return to my home from which I came.' [25]But upon returning, it finds it swept clean and put in order. [26]Then it goes and brings back seven other spirits more wicked than itself who move in and dwell there, and the last condition of that person is worse than the first."

True Blessedness. [27]While he was speaking, a woman from the crowd called out and said to him, "Blessed is the womb that carried you and the breasts at which you nursed." [28]He replied, "Rather, blessed are those who hear the word of God and observe it."

must first tie up the strong man, Luke states that someone must overcome or be victorious over the strong man (11:22). There has been evidence of victory all along in the Lukan text.

11:24-26 The return of the evil spirit

Luke sees the contest with Satan as a real battle, and the enemy does not relinquish control easily. The house to which the seven other evil spirits return is the same good one from which the unclean spirit had previously departed. Their roaming through "arid regions searching for rest" stands as a metaphor for those people who do not fill their lives with the goodness of God. Nature abhors a vacuum, and thus seven other wicked spirits find a home within the now empty individual (v. 26). This understanding can be applied to Judas, about whom Luke states that Satan "enter[s]" (22:3). Judas never allowed into his heart the grace that Jesus brings, and thus the wicked spirits take up residence there.

In Luke's Gospel, the battle between Christ and Satan, announced at the birth (1:78-79), begins at the temptation (4:1-13). Jesus has been waging and winning battles against the devil demons all along, but Christ's ultimate victory over Satan, a victory of light over darkness, will come at the cross. This theme continues in the Acts of the Apostles.

11:27-28 True blessedness

The narrative flow forms a juxtaposition of seeming opposites. After the long deliberation about Beelzebul, the strong man, and unclean spirits, a woman in the crowd turns the subject to blessedness, and does so by making a reference to Jesus' mother. Jesus' response, however, demonstrates that his call goes beyond natural kinship; indeed, natural kinship might even be an impediment (see 8:19-21).

The Demand for a Sign. ²⁹While still more people gathered in the crowd, he said to them, "This generation is an evil generation; it seeks a sign, but no sign will be given it, except the sign of Jonah. ³⁰Just as Jonah became a sign to the Ninevites, so will the Son of Man be to this generation. ³¹At the judgment the queen of the south will rise with the men of this generation and she will condemn them, because she came from the ends of the earth to hear the wisdom of Solomon, and there is something greater than Solomon here. ³²At the judgment the men of Nineveh will arise with this generation and condemn it, because at the preaching of Jonah they repented,

---

11:29-32 The demand for a sign

Luke avoids redundancy. The narrative sequence has already informed the reader that people are testing and arguing with Jesus (see Luke 11:15), so, unlike Matthew and Mark (12:38; 8:11-12), Luke does not mention Pharisees or scribes badgering Jesus. Jesus simply continues with his teaching.

The book of Jonah forms the necessary background for any interpretation of this passage. The Lukan text in verse 30 is helpful in this regard by supplying the central element of that particular Old Testament work. That Nineveh was the ancient capital of the Assyrians, the people who ravaged the Israelite kingdom under Shalmaneser V in 722 B.C., sharpens the drama of the Jonah story. Jonah is the son of Amittai. Amittai is also the name of one of the prophets from the time of King Jeroboam II (786–746 B.C.). If the name Amittai refers to one and the same person, then it would have been understood that Jonah came from the Israelite kingdom just as the Assyrian Empire was menacing it.

Jonah is sent on a mission, therefore, into absolutely alien and hostile territory, to a land feared and despised by all his compatriots. After fits and starts, including a sojourn in the belly of a great fish (Jonah 2:1), Jonah reaches his destination and preaches judgment, with the result that the whole city of Nineveh, from the king to the lowliest beast, repents. This repentance is the sign of Jonah to which Luke refers in verses 29-30. The explanation continues.

In verse 31 Luke also has a reference to "the queen of the south," or the Queen of Sheba (see 1 Kgs 10:1ff.; 2 Chr 9:1ff.; Matt 12:42). With this allusion the lesson works in reverse: the pagan makes the journey to the land of the true God. In both cases nonbelievers make acts of repentance or faith. Jesus draws a comparison and contrast between those within and those outside the pale of revelation, and in so doing, proclaims the wide

and there is something greater than Jonah here.

The Simile of Light. ³³"No one who lights a lamp hides it away or places it [under a bushel basket], but on a lampstand so that those who enter might see the light. ³⁴The lamp of the body is your eye. When your eye is sound, then your whole body is filled with light, but when it is bad, then your body is in darkness. ³⁵Take care, then, that the light in you not become darkness. ³⁶If your whole body is full of light, and no part of it is in darkness, then it will be as full of light as a lamp illuminating you with its brightness."

Denunciation of the Pharisees and Scholars of the Law. ³⁷After he had spoken, a Pharisee invited him to dine at his home. He entered and reclined at table to eat. ³⁸The Pharisee was amazed to see that he did not observe the prescribed washing before the meal. ³⁹The Lord said to him, "Oh you Pharisees! Although you cleanse the outside of the cup and the dish, inside you are filled with plunder and evil. ⁴⁰You fools! Did not the maker of the outside also make the inside? ⁴¹But as to what is within, give alms, and behold, everything will be clean for you. ⁴²Woe to you Pharisees! You pay tithes of mint and of rue and of every garden herb, but you pay no attention to judgment and to love for God. These you should have done, without overlooking the

invitation of God's love and salvation as well as the breadth of human response to it. In the end Jonah, with his example of the Ninevites, and the queen of the south, with her pilgrimage to Solomon, will stand in judgment of those who reject Jesus.

11:33-36 The visibility of light

These verses are a reprise of the lamp motif seen in 8:16ff. Luke elaborates the analogy here. The discourses about Jonah and the queen of the south in verses 30-31 above provide the example of how "lights" and "lamps" can further evangelization. Matthew uses this Q material as well but places it at two different locations within the Sermon on the Mount (5:13-16 and 6:22-23). Luke, on the other hand, finishes this section with a wonderful simile for a true disciple. The Christian life involves the whole body and all human action. The way people conduct themselves determines the persons they will become. Filled with faith, these people, by their brightness will lead others from darkness into the light of faith. The light and darkness dichotomy in this Q material is reminiscent of John's Gospel.

11:37-54 Denunciation of the legal experts

This section, called the "Woes," has a parallel in Matthew 23:1-38. Differences between the two can be seen in Matthew's concern for and

others. [43]Woe to you Pharisees! You love the seat of honor in synagogues and greetings in marketplaces. [44]Woe to you! You are like unseen graves over which people unknowingly walk."

[45]Then one of the scholars of the law said to him in reply, "Teacher, by saying this you are insulting us too." [46]And he said, "Woe also to you scholars of the law! You impose on people burdens hard to carry, but you yourselves do not lift one finger to touch them. [47]Woe to you! You build the memorials of the prophets whom your ancestors killed. [48]Consequently, you bear witness and give consent to the deeds of your ancestors, for they killed them and you do the building. [49]Therefore, the wisdom of God said, 'I will send to them prophets and apostles; some of them they will kill and persecute' [50]in order that this generation might be charged with the blood of all the prophets shed since the foundation of the world, [51]from the blood of Abel to the blood of Zechariah who died between the altar and the temple building. Yes, I tell you, this generation will be charged with their blood! [52]Woe to you, scholars of the law! You have taken away the key of knowledge. You yourselves did not enter and you stopped those trying to enter." [53]When he left, the scribes and Pharisees began to act with hostility toward him and to interrogate him about many things, [54]for they were plotting to catch him at something he might say.

---

knowledge of the Law, something that Luke, in writing for a Gentile audience, has no need to address.

The Pharisee literally invites Jesus to breakfast, indicated by the Greek verb *aristáō*. If Palestinian social customs of ancient times are in any way similar to those today, the breakfast would be quite substantial and would be taken around ten o'clock in the morning, but it would not be the main meal of the day, which is taken in the evening. The fact that Pharisees and scholars take issue with Jesus in the manner that they do exposes an ulterior motive: they wish to observe his behavior with hopes of gaining evidence against him. If they had really wished to honor him, they would have invited him for the evening repast. Jesus recognizes this plot and responds by revealing their true motives in front of all. He also exhibits the shallowness and hypocrisy of their deeds. Jesus' denunciation at verses 47-51 foreshadows his own death. The system that killed the prophets will also, by implication, kill him, as verses 53-54 substantiate.

It is difficult to identify which Zechariah (v. 51) Luke is referring to. Many see him as Zechariah the priest, son of Jehoiadah (see 2 Chr 24:20-22). Others have seen him as Zechariah the priest, the father of John the Baptist.

12 The Leaven of the Pharisees.

¹Meanwhile, so many people were crowding together that they were trampling one another underfoot. He began to speak, first to his disciples, "Beware of the leaven—that is, the hypocrisy—of the Pharisees.

Courage under Persecution. ²"There is nothing concealed that will not be revealed, nor secret that will not be known. ³Therefore whatever you have said in the darkness will be heard in the light, and what you have whispered behind closed doors will be proclaimed on the housetops. ⁴I tell you, my friends, do not be afraid of those who kill the body but after that can do no more. ⁵I shall show you whom to fear. Be afraid of the one who after killing has the power to cast into Gehenna;

12:1-12 In face of persecution

We last read of the crowds in 11:29. Mention of them here returns our focus to Jesus' preaching. The reference to the "leaven . . . of the Pharisees" (v. 1) thematically connects this scene with the meal at the Pharisee's house (11:27-54).

In verse 4 Jesus calls his disciples, and possibly by extension the rest of the people, "friends." This is the only occurrence in all three Synoptic Gospels in which we see this form of address applied to Jesus' followers, and it is another example of a tradition Luke seems to share with John (see John 15:14-15).

In a time of persecution, people generally go into hiding and maintain a secret existence. Jesus' admonition describes a situation in which no hiding will be possible, even if it were desirable. True fear should be reserved for the One who can cast a believer into Gehenna after the body is dead (v. 5). This phrase serves as a circumlocution emphasizing that we need fear only God.

"Gehenna" is a Greek transliteration of the Hebrew *Hinnom*, the name of the valley on the western side of Jerusalem. Often cursed by the Jewish prophets for the child sacrifice that the Jerusalemites practiced there, it is also called Topheth (see 2 Kgs 23:10; Jer 7:31-32; 19:6, 11-14). In time, the Valley of Hinnom functioned as the city garbage dump, thereby making it ritually unclean. In both Jewish and Christian canonical and deuterocanonical texts, Gehenna is the metaphor for hell. As Jesus makes plain in other parts of his ministry, we have a hand in determining our salvation by opting to participate in God's grace. He emphasizes that our salvation lies beyond the reach of any persecutor.

Not even denying Christ in the face of danger and threat will bring eternal condemnation; only a sin against the holy Spirit has that power.

yes, I tell you, be afraid of that one. ⁶Are not five sparrows sold for two small coins? Yet not one of them has escaped the notice of God. ⁷Even the hairs of your head have all been counted. Do not be afraid. You are worth more than many sparrows. ⁸I tell you, everyone who acknowledges me before others the Son of Man will acknowledge before the angels of God. ⁹But whoever denies me before others will be denied before the angels of God.

Sayings about the holy Spirit. ¹⁰"Everyone who speaks a word against the Son of Man will be forgiven, but the one who blasphemes against the holy Spirit will not be forgiven. ¹¹When they take you before synagogues and before rulers and authorities, do not worry about how or what your defense will be or about what you are to say. ¹²For the holy Spirit will teach you at that moment what you should say."

Saying against Greed. ¹³Someone in the crowd said to him, "Teacher, tell my brother to share the inheritance with me." ¹⁴He replied to him, "Friend, who appointed me as your judge and arbitrator?" ¹⁵Then he said to the crowd,

---

The sin against the holy Spirit is the refusal of God's mercy and forgiveness when it is offered. Here, too, by having the choice to accept or reject the love of Christ, we have a role in determining our salvation.

God will not abandon those facing the sword. The holy Spirit will not only be present in fortifying the witnesses to Jesus but will also direct them in their actions and speak on their behalf, as Luke demonstrates in the Acts of the Apostles.

12:13-21 Greed and riches

This section consists of a dialogue followed by a parable. The first half, prompted by someone in the crowd calling out to Jesus, succinctly presents Jesus' true role and ministry while offering an ethical and eschatological lesson.

The person who calls out from the crowd misunderstands Jesus' mission. The person errs by viewing Jesus as an arbiter whose judgment rests on interpreting the intricacies of a legal code. Jesus refuses to be cast in such a position, and he turns the table on the questioner as well as the brother. The issue, Jesus implies, is not who is right or wrong about the inheritance; it is about greed and avarice. If both exhibited less covetousness, one would be inclined to share with the other, and the other would not suspect that he was being cheated. Jesus' ministry is to the lost, and both brothers are sinners. His action allows the two to receive his message. No one loses, and both have the opportunity to enter the kingdom. The parable of the rich fool, which follows (vv. 16-21), illustrates the lesson.

"Take care to guard against all greed, for though one may be rich, one's life does not consist of possessions."

Parable of the Rich Fool. ¹⁶Then he told them a parable. "There was a rich man whose land produced a bountiful harvest. ¹⁷He asked himself, 'What shall I do, for I do not have space to store my harvest?' ¹⁸And he said, 'This is what I shall do: I shall tear down my barns and build larger ones. There I shall store all my grain and other goods ¹⁹and I shall say to myself, "Now as for you, you have so many good things stored up for many years, rest, eat, drink, be merry!"' ²⁰But God said to him, 'You fool, this night your life will be demanded of you; and the things you have prepared, to whom will they belong?' ²¹Thus will it be for the one who stores up treasure for himself but is not rich in what matters to God."

Dependence on God. ²²He said to [his] disciples, "Therefore I tell you, do not worry about your life and what you will eat, or about your body and what you will wear. ²³For life is more than food and the body more than clothing. ²⁴Notice the ravens: they do not sow or reap; they have neither storehouse nor

At no point in his discourse does the rich fool credit God for the harvest. Furthermore, he never acknowledges that the bounty should have some purpose other than satisfying his own desires. Because he is so selfish and self-centered, he dies without benefit of both his wealth and God's love. With this parable, Jesus warns the two brothers to guard against ending up like the rich fool—a total loser. An example of how bad it will be for someone like this individual is found in the parable of the rich man and Lazarus (16:19-31).

12:22-34 Trust and faith in God

Matthew places this discourse within the Sermon on the Mount (see Matt 6:25-34), while Luke situates it on the journey to Jerusalem. Nonetheless, the lesson is the same: God's love is so abundant that he looks after every human need. In Luke, this passage provides the proper frame of mind and heart that stands in contrast to the focus of the rich fool seen above (vv. 16-21).

The Greek *korax,* translated here as "ravens" (v. 24), can also mean "crow"; in any case, it refers to a scavenger. Not only was such a creature forbidden as food to Jews, but it was considered a disgusting bird also among Gentile Greeks. Its repulsive character, therefore, makes the comparison all the more striking. Using the rhetorical form of the comparison of the greater, the listener or reader understands that if God tends to the needs of a repugnant carrion-eater, how much more will he care for his beloved people (see also Ps 147:9 and Job 38:41).

barn, yet God feeds them. How much more important are you than birds! [25]Can any of you by worrying add a moment to your lifespan? [26]If even the smallest things are beyond your control, why are you anxious about the rest? [27]Notice how the flowers grow. They do not toil or spin. But I tell you, not even Solomon in all his splendor was dressed like one of them. [28]If God so clothes the grass in the field that grows today and is thrown into the oven tomorrow, will he not much more provide for you, O you of little faith? [29]As for you, do not seek what you are to eat and what you are to drink, and do not worry anymore. [30]All the nations of the world seek for these things, and your Father knows that you need them. [31]Instead, seek his kingdom, and these other things will be given you besides. [32]Do not be afraid any longer, little flock, for your Father is pleased to give you the kingdom. [33]Sell your belongings and give alms. Provide money bags for yourselves that do not wear out, an inexhaustible treasure in heaven that no thief can reach nor moth destroy. [34]For where your treasure is, there also will your heart be.

Vigilant and Faithful Servants. [35]"Gird your loins and light your lamps [36]and be like servants who await their master's return from a wedding, ready to open immediately when he comes and knocks. [37]Blessed are those servants

---

This same type of comparison is employed further on in the passage with the flowers, called *krinon* in Greek. Most probably it is the crocus, referred to in other parts of the Bible as the "rose of Sharon" (Song 2:1). Against the green Galilean hillsides in rainy times of the year, these blossoms give a dazzling appearance. Yet the spectacular color of the grass and flowers is short-lived. As soon as the weather turns warm, both the herbage and the blooms shrivel up. In a land with little wood, dried grass is often used for fuel. Once again we hear the comparison of the greater. If God shows so much attention to what ends up in the fire, how much more does he care for his people.

Luke introduces a social justice theme not paralleled in Matthew's version. The "inexhaustible treasure in heaven" (v. 33) comes from almsgiving. Luke underscores the lesson of the discourse with verse 34. If we make ourselves rich in the eyes of God, our hearts and motivation will lead to union with God both in this life and the life to come. Furthermore, by becoming rich in heaven, we relieve ourselves of earthly anxiety.

12:35-48 The need for vigilance

The metaphors for vigilance all make the same point: the Lord's coming, or parousia, will happen when we least expect it. Each of the examples, however, gives a variety of views of what one can expect.

whom the master finds vigilant on his arrival. Amen, I say to you, he will gird himself, have them recline at table, and proceed to wait on them. ³⁸And should he come in the second or third watch and find them prepared in this way, blessed are those servants. ³⁹Be sure of this: if the master of the house had known the hour when the thief was coming, he would not have let his house be broken into. ⁴⁰You also must be prepared, for at an hour you do not expect, the Son of Man will come."

⁴¹Then Peter said, "Lord, is this parable meant for us or for everyone?" ⁴²And the Lord replied, "Who, then, is the faithful and prudent steward whom the master will put in charge of his servants to distribute [the] food allowance at the proper time? ⁴³Blessed is that servant whom his master on arrival finds doing so. ⁴⁴Truly, I say to you, he will put him in charge of all his property. ⁴⁵But if that servant says to himself, 'My master is delayed in coming,' and begins to beat the menservants and the maidservants, to eat and drink and get drunk, ⁴⁶then that servant's master will come on an unexpected day and at an unknown hour and will punish him severely and assign him a place with the unfaithful.

A master returning from a wedding would come with his bride (vv. 35-38). There would be feasting and celebration associated with the homecoming, which the servants should be ready to facilitate. In a role reversal, this master serves the servants. So too will it be at the eschatological banquet, when Jesus will be the host. The Lord's coming will arrive with the shock and surprise of a nighttime thief breaking into a house.

The notion of preparation introduces a paradox: this passage seems to contradict the parable of the rich fool (12:16-21). There readers are told not to worry about the morrow, food, or clothing, but here they are admonished not to take anything for granted, but to be ready for the unexpected. The paradox lies in the fact that adequate preparation is the result of letting go of worldly concerns and values. The prepared person will not be attached to the concerns of this life, even though she may be immersed in the midst of them.

The parable of the wise and just servant likewise has a strain of irony running through it (vv. 42-48). A good foreman will not take advantage of those under him, and if he does, the master will depose him upon his return. Such a punishment, however, is reserved only for the servant who knew his master's will and acted shamefully. The servant who does not know the master's will and commits the same actions will get off with a lighter punishment. The parable is a lesson in discipleship that parallels Luke 19:11-27. Followers of Christ will be held to a higher standard than nonbelievers.

47That servant who knew his master's will but did not make preparations nor act in accord with his will shall be beaten severely; 48and the servant who was ignorant of his master's will but acted in a way deserving of a severe beating shall be beaten only lightly. Much will be required of the person entrusted with much, and still more will be demanded of the person entrusted with more.

◄ **Jesus: A Cause of Division.** 49"I have come to set the earth on fire, and how I
◄ wish it were already blazing! 50There is a baptism with which I must be baptized, and how great is my anguish until it is accomplished! 51Do you think that I have come to establish peace on the earth? No, I tell you, but rather division. 52From now on a household of five will be divided, three against two and two against three; 53a father will be divided against his son and a son against his father, a mother against her daughter and a daughter against her mother, a mother-in-law against her daughter-in-law and a daughter-in-law against her mother-in-law."

12:49-59 Division, signs, conduct

Although this section appears to come from Q, verses 49-50 are found only in Luke's Gospel. The evangelist wishes to underscore that discipleship is not without its price, and the world will not gladly welcome the kingdom of God. Fire and water are both elements of destruction and cleansing, and as harsh as the imagery may seem, Luke uses them here to show the immediacy and totality of the impending *eschaton*. The more specific examples of how Christ's message will be received (vv. 51-53) depict a situation in the early church, most probably within the Jewish-Christian synagogues from which the Christians were eventually expelled.

In Israel and Palestine, rain can only come from the Mediterranean and only in the winter, hence the reference to the west wind (v. 54). Similarly, the Sahara, Sinai, and Arabian deserts lie in the south and are the source of the hot, desiccating breeze (v. 55). The signs of the times should be just as obvious.

This discourse works on several levels. The historical signs are the political precariousness of the Jewish state during the intertestamental epoch: Roman occupation, political dissension, and corrupt administration threatened the society to the point of anarchy. On the religious front, the signs of the times were Jesus' ministry (see Luke 4:16-21). These signs are the same no matter what the period in history. Issues of social justice coupled with the religious and spiritual emptiness are signs pointing to the eschatological reign. The Christian is called to respond to them.

The section ends with instruction to the early Christian community itself (vv. 57-59). As a people baptized in Christ's name, they should settle

Signs of the Times. ⁵⁴He also said to the crowds, "When you see [a] cloud rising in the west you say immediately that it is going to rain—and so it does; ⁵⁵and when you notice that the wind is blowing from the south you say that it is going to be hot—and so it is. ⁵⁶You hypocrites! You know how to interpret the appearance of the earth and the sky; why do you not know how to interpret the present time?

Settlement with an Opponent. ⁵⁷"Why do you not judge for yourselves what is right? ⁵⁸If you are to go with your opponent before a magistrate, make an effort to settle the matter on the way; otherwise your opponent will turn you over to the judge, and the judge hand you over to the constable, and the constable throw you into prison. ⁵⁹I say to you, you will not be released until you have paid the last penny."

13 A Call to Repentance. ¹At that time some people who were present there told him about the Galileans whose blood Pilate had mingled with the blood of their sacrifices. ²He said to them in reply, "Do you think that because these Galileans suffered in this way they were greater sinners than all other Galileans? ³By no means! But I tell you, if you do not repent, you will all perish as they did! ⁴Or those eighteen people who were killed when the tower at Siloam fell on them—do you

---

differences within the community and not resort to the pagan law courts. Christians have a new standard of behavior that encompasses personal behavior as well as ways of resolving injustices. These standards extend beyond restitution and include mercy, redemption, and forgiveness. Such an interpretation does not mean covering up shameful or wrongful behavior behind a cloak of secrecy; rather, it means making the community a living symbol of justice and reconciliation (see Matt 5:25-26).

13:1-9 Sin and repentance

The incident involving Pilate referred to here is one of the few places where he is mentioned outside the passion narratives, and it is very telling.

Many see Pontius Pilate as a weak, vacillating governor who feels overwhelmed by the vagaries of the mob, and, against his better judgment, he hands Jesus over to be crucified (see Matt 27:26; Mark 15:15; Luke 23:25; John 19:16). Luke's narrative counters such an assessment by relating this slaughter, for which there is no other record in the Bible or any other extant work. Josephus refers to an uprising of Jews when Pilate uses temple money to build a Jerusalem aqueduct (*Ant.* 18.3.2 and *J.W.* 2.9.4). Pilate ruthlessly suppresses the tumult by having disguised, weapon-bearing Roman soldiers mixed among the Jews. At a given signal, they begin to hack away at the civilian population.

think they were more guilty than everyone else who lived in Jerusalem? [5]By no means! But I tell you, if you do not repent, you will all perish as they did!"

The Parable of the Barren Fig Tree. [6]And he told them this parable: "There once was a person who had a fig tree planted in his orchard, and when he came in search of fruit on it but found none, [7]he said to the gardener, 'For three years now I have come in search of fruit on this fig tree but have found none. [So] cut it down. Why should it exhaust the soil?' [8]He said to him in reply, 'Sir, leave it for this year also, and I shall cultivate the ground around it and fertilize it; [9]it may bear fruit in the future. If not you can cut it down.'"

It is quite plausible that both Josephus and Jesus are referring to the same calamity. Likewise, along the southeastern wall of ancient Jerusalem are visible ruins from a collapsed tower (v. 4) dating to the intertestamental period, that is, the two centuries between the composition of the last book of the Old Testament and the first book of the New Testament.

The lesson that Jesus draws from these events releases human suffering from the capricious judgment of wrathful gods, where many of then contemporary pagan cults had placed it, or even from known or unknown sinful behavior, as many in the Jewish religious establishment then taught. Instead, Jesus is saying that suffering comes to good and bad alike, and that all humankind stands in need of repentance and redemption. Someone's misfortune is not an indicator of moral culpability. John's Gospel (9:2) features a similar lesson in the healing of the person born blind (see also Ps 7:12-13).

With the parable of the fig tree (vv. 6-9), Luke employs a graceful thematic continuity from the stress on repentance to the value of the sinner. The fig tree is highly prized for the luscious texture and sweetness of its fruit (see Judg 9:10-11; 1 Kgs 5:5; 2 Kgs 18:31). Furthermore, the fruit can be dried and preserved for years on end.

The inedible variety of figs looks exactly like the edible kind. Moreover, edible figs can only be pollinated by the female fig wasp (*Blastophaga psenes*), which carries the pollen from the inedible fig and burrows into the buds of the edible one. Hence, for proper cultivation both types of fig trees are necessary. This delicate operation can confuse even the best gardeners, and patience is necessary to ensure a good harvest of the precious fruit. The lesson is that God will not give up on those who struggle with turning toward him. In addition, the great value placed on the fig tree characterizes the value of the sinner in God's eyes—not a reprobate or an outcast, but a prized possession, despite the possibility that the sinner may never "bear fruit."

Cure of a Crippled Woman on the Sabbath. ¹⁰He was teaching in a synagogue on the sabbath. ¹¹And a woman was there who for eighteen years had been crippled by a spirit; she was bent over, completely incapable of standing erect. ¹²When Jesus saw her, he called to her and said, "Woman, you are set free of your infirmity." ¹³He laid his hands on her, and she at once stood up straight and glorified God. ¹⁴But the leader of the synagogue, indignant that Jesus had cured on the sabbath, said to the crowd in reply, "There are six days when work should be done. Come on those days to be cured, not on the sabbath day." ¹⁵The Lord said to him in reply, "Hypocrites! Does not each one of you on the sabbath untie his ox or his ass from the manger and lead it out for watering? ¹⁶This daughter of Abraham, whom Satan has bound for eighteen years now, ought she not to have been set free on the sabbath day from this bondage?" ¹⁷When

---

13:10-17 The cure of the crippled woman on the sabbath

If Jesus was teaching in the synagogue, he must have originally met with respect from the synagogue leader. In fact, the leader reprimands not Jesus but the crowd of people who seemingly have come on the sabbath to be cured. The cause of the leader's discomfort, therefore, is not that Jesus cured but that this curing occurred on the Lord's Day. Healing was seen as work and therefore prohibited. Jesus uses this opportunity to make several points about his identity, his reign, and the world.

The Jewish sabbath, since it commemorates the seventh day on which God rested from all his labors, is literally the Lord's Day. Because of the holy character of the sabbath, the regulations against work were intended to give everyone access to this life in the Lord. Judging from Jesus' response, it appears that in this situation, the sabbath regulations had ceased to provide the spiritual renewal that originally had been associated with them. Jesus' challenge to the custom is successful only because of his authority. He thus gives the sabbath an eschatological dimension. Access to life in the Lord now becomes a foretaste of the heavenly realm, where sin and suffering are put to rout. This interpretation is evident in Jesus' reply (v. 16).

The reference to Satan in verse 16, combined with the setting of the cure on the sabbath, characterizes a central aspect of Lukan eschatology. Sickness and malady are viewed as a part of Satan's malevolent realm, which has made inroads into God's creation. Jesus' role is to redeem creation, to win it back for God. Jesus overpowers the evil forces and ushers in the eschatological reign. No longer dominated by Satan, the crippled woman now has her sabbath rest.

93

he said this, all his adversaries were humiliated; and the whole crowd rejoiced at all the splendid deeds done by him.

The Parable of the Mustard Seed. [18]Then he said, "What is the kingdom of God like? To what can I compare it? [19]It is like a mustard seed that a person took and planted in the garden. When it was fully grown, it became a large bush and 'the birds of the sky dwelt in its branches.'"

The Parable of the Yeast. [20]Again he said, "To what shall I compare the kingdom of God? [21]It is like yeast that a woman took and mixed [in] with three measures of wheat flour until the whole batch of dough was leavened."

The Narrow Door; Salvation and Rejection. [22]He passed through towns and villages, teaching as he went and making his way to Jerusalem. [23]Someone asked him, "Lord, will only a few people

13:18-19 The parable of the mustard seed

All three Synoptics show this parable. The mustard seed was considered the smallest of all possible seeds. The tree itself, the *brassica nigra*, grows wild throughout Palestine and Israel, but farmers also cultivate it. With small, bright yellow flowers and slender, dark green leaves, it can grow to a large, many-branched shrub or tree. As such, it is a metaphor for the small early Christian community, which has an influence on the world going far beyond its size and number to the point that others (symbolized by birds) make their home in it.

13:20-21 The measure of yeast

This parable appears only in Matthew and Luke. The bread of the time would have been sourdough, as most bread was until the development of dry yeast. Once the dough was kneaded, pieces were pulled away, flattened, and laid over a hot metal dome called a *tamboun*. The result was a large, circular crêpe or pita.

Not much yeast was needed to cause a batch of dough to rise, so, like the parable of the mustard seed, the leaven stands as a measure for the Christian community. In this parable the woman who adds the yeast to the flour is the Christ figure.

13:22-30 The narrow door, salvation, and rejection

With this parable Jesus indirectly answers the question put to him. Restrictions to entering the kingdom do not lie with God but with the human response to the divine invitation. Because Luke recapitulates the point that Jesus is on his way to Jerusalem (v. 22), many consider this section as the beginning of the second half of the journey narrative leading to the city of his death and resurrection.

be saved?" He answered them, ²⁴"Strive to enter through the narrow gate, for many, I tell you, will attempt to enter but will not be strong enough. ²⁵After the master of the house has arisen and locked the door, then will you stand outside knocking and saying, 'Lord, open the door for us.' He will say to you in reply, 'I do not know where you are from.' ²⁶And you will say, 'We ate and drank in your company and you taught in our streets.' ²⁷Then he will say to you, 'I do not know where [you] are from. Depart from me, all you evildoers!' ²⁸And there will be wailing and grinding of teeth when you see Abraham, Isaac, and Jacob and all the prophets in the kingdom of God and you yourselves cast out. ²⁹And people will come from the east and the west and from the north and the south and will recline at table in the kingdom of God. ³⁰For behold, some are last who will be first, and some are first who will be last."

The conventional city gate during this period had one wide, high central arch flanked by two lower, narrower portals. The main arch permitted camels, carts, and goods to pass. Those who wished to enter and who had no baggage trains could avoid the traffic by walking through either one of the narrow gates.

Applying this daily occurrence to the parable, the lesson seems to be directed to those who drag along their religious or social status, their material possessions, or their own ambitions in seeking easy access to salvation. Jesus counters this attitude by extracting a lesson from a familiar scene. Just as today those who travel light reach their destination more easily than those with much luggage, so too will those who keep their eyes and actions on salvation find the swifter path through the smaller doors. Any attempt to interpret these verses as showing that Gentiles are saved at the expense of the Jews is based on a faulty reading. The setting of the story is Jesus' trip to Jerusalem accompanied by his Jewish disciples, but the Lukan community to whom this story is told is composed mostly of Gentiles. All are instructed, therefore, to enter by the narrow gate, a passage that is difficult but not impossible.

The introduction of mixed metaphors in verses 25-30 is a result of various strands of tradition redacted into one parable. The second lesson is similar to the first: one should not rely on status to enter the kingdom. To use a modern parallel, ticket holders who arrive for a concert at the last minute may still not get in if there is a long line at the gate; their reliance on their ticket stubs proves to be no guarantee of entry. If they had been earnest in their desire, they would have arrived early and waited in line to be sure of getting a seat.

Herod's Desire to Kill Jesus. ³¹At that time some Pharisees came to him and said, "Go away, leave this area because Herod wants to kill you." ³²He replied, "Go and tell that fox, 'Behold, I cast out demons and I perform healings today and tomorrow, and on the third day I accomplish my purpose. ³³Yet I must continue on my way today, tomorrow, and the following day, for it is impossible that a prophet should die outside of Jerusalem.'

The Lament over Jerusalem. ³⁴"Jerusalem, Jerusalem, you who kill the prophets and stone those sent to you, how many times I yearned to gather your children together as a hen gathers her brood under her wings, but you were unwilling! ³⁵Behold, your house will be abandoned. [But] I tell you, you

13:31-33 The Pharisees warn about Herod

Do the Pharisees come to Jesus as friends and allies, or are they simply trying to frighten Jesus into submission? In either case, Jesus does not alter his intention to head to Jerusalem. Indeed, he uses the occasion to affirm it—he must go to Jerusalem (v. 33).

Lukan eschatology once again surfaces with the blending of three statements in verse 32. As in the parable of the crippled woman (13:10-17), curing the sick is seen as a successful assault on demonic forces. Furthermore, contained in this statement is a reference to Jesus' passion, death, and resurrection: "On the third day I accomplish my purpose" (v. 32). Jesus predicts his own death with his emphatic resolution to continue to Jerusalem, though, ironically, by traveling to Jerusalem he leaves Herod's jurisdiction.

13:34-35 The lament over Jerusalem

This passage, a rhetorical apostrophe, flows from the scene with the Pharisees immediately above and is a fine example of Luke's narrative finesse. Matthew's Gospel contains a parallel account, but in that Gospel Jesus utters these words after the triumphant entry into Jerusalem (see Matt 23:37-39).

In 13:33 Jesus says that a prophet should not die outside Jerusalem. His words over the city have him identifying with that destiny, and he does so by using a lament, a prophetic genre seen most clearly in Jeremiah and Lamentations. To be sure, prophets were also slain outside Jerusalem, but given the presence of the temple within the city and the city's history with the prophets, Jeremiah and Isaiah make Jerusalem the major symbol of a prophet's destiny (see 1 Kgs 9:7-8; 2 Kgs 21:16; Ps 118:2; Jer 22:5).

In verse 34 the reader should note the feminine imagery inherent in Jesus' self-referential term "hen" (see also Deut 32:11). Contained also is the allusion to his entering the city in 19:28-40.

will not see me until [the time comes when] you say, 'Blessed is he who comes in the name of the Lord.'"

14 **Healing of the Man with Dropsy on the Sabbath.** ¹On a sabbath he went to dine at the home of one of the leading Pharisees, and the people there were observing him carefully. ²In front of him there was a man suffering from dropsy. ³Jesus spoke to the scholars of the law and Pharisees in reply, asking, "Is it lawful to cure on the sabbath or not?" ⁴But they kept silent; so he took the man and, after he had healed him, dismissed him. ⁵Then he said to them, "Who among you, if your son or ox falls into a cistern, would not immediately pull him out on the sabbath day?" ⁶But they were unable to answer his question.

Conduct of Invited Guests and Hosts. ⁷He told a parable to those who had been invited, noticing how they were choosing the places of honor at the table. ⁸"When you are invited by someone to a wedding banquet, do not

---

14:1-6 Healing a man with dropsy on the sabbath

Dropsy, or edema, is characterized by a buildup of fluids, often in the extremities. It is usually symptomatic of a variety of diseases.

There are several similarities between this story and the account of the crippled woman (13:10-17). They are solely Lukan material, and in both cases the miracle occurs on the sabbath. The woman is cured in front of the synagogue leaders, and the man here is restored to health in the presence of leading Pharisees. Furthermore, neither the woman nor the man asks Jesus to be healed; rather, in both instances Jesus, moved by pity, takes the initiative to cure the individual. He explains his action using the rhetorical device of the comparison of the greater: if the Law makes allowances for saving livestock on the sabbath, how much more should one help a fellow human being on the holy day.

Unlike the passage about the woman, however, there is nothing in this story to indicate that the leaders were angry or that they had duplicitous intentions in "observing him carefully" (v.1). It seems that the Pharisees here are indeed curious about how Jesus would handle such a case, and, he engages them with his question (v. 3). Because they, too, know the Law and its provisions, they remain silent. Once again, the sabbath setting connects physical well-being with eternal salvation, thereby giving the Lord's Day an eschatological dimension (see also Luke 6:1-11; 11:37-54).

14:7-14 Proper comportment of guests and hosts

With the man now cured of his dropsy, Luke continues to describe the action surrounding the dinner. Jesus observes the customs of courtesy and etiquette and ties these issues of daily protocol to a lesson about the kingdom.

recline at table in the place of honor. A more distinguished guest than you may have been invited by him, [9]and the host who invited both of you may approach you and say, 'Give your place to this man,' and then you would proceed with embarrassment to take the lowest place. [10]Rather, when you are invited, go and take the lowest place so that when the host comes to you he may say, 'My friend, move up to a higher position.' Then you will enjoy the esteem of your companions at the table. [11]For everyone who exalts himself will be humbled, but the one who humbles himself will be exalted." [12]Then he said to the host who invited him, "When you hold a lunch or a dinner, do not invite your friends or your brothers or your relatives or your wealthy neighbors, in case they may invite you back and you have repayment. [13]Rather, when you hold a banquet, in-

---

Luke calls this lesson a "parable" (v. 7), but its genre is closer to a wisdom saying. Only Luke contains this passage, although a parallel to verse 11 appears in Matthew 23:12, making this aphorism most probably a Q saying. It is also found in Luke 18:14.

The dining room would have been a *triclinium* (see 7:36-50). The host would recline on his left side at the top of the right extension of the table; the opening to the horseshoe-shaped construction would have been to his back. The place of honor would have been at the crossbar, making the position of the honored guest directly perpendicular to the host so that they could talk directly to each other. Succeeding places of honor continued along the crossbar and down the left side, with the lowest place situated at the end of the left extension; the guest would have to constantly readjust his position in order to converse with those in the lowest places. What Jesus notices, therefore, is a stream of guests jockeying for the spot perpendicular to the host while avoiding anything along the left extension, especially the last place.

In the Mediterranean world, an honor-shame based culture, the social gaffe of overstepping one's station, such as Jesus describes, would have been a mortifying experience. On the other hand, being asked to come higher would have been particularly enviable. The lesson goes beyond calculating a social standing among one's peers, however, and points to the proper disposition toward God and how we define our need for God's salvation in our lives. Social self-inflation is equated with spiritual self-righteousness. Those who assume that they are righteous enough to let themselves into the kingdom without any regard for the divine initiative will have to give way to those who know their unworthiness and depend on God's love and grace for everything.

vite the poor, the crippled, the lame, the blind; [14]blessed indeed will you be because of their inability to repay you. For you will be repaid at the resurrection of the righteous."

The Parable of the Great Feast. [15]One of his fellow guests on hearing this said to him, "Blessed is the one who will dine in the kingdom of God." [16]He replied to him, "A man gave a great dinner to which he invited many. [17]When the time for the dinner came, he dispatched his servant to say to those invited, 'Come, everything is now ready.' [18]But one by one, they all began to excuse themselves. The first said to him, 'I have purchased a field and must go to examine it; I ask you, consider me excused.' [19]And another said, 'I have purchased five yoke of oxen and am on my way to evaluate them; I ask you, consider me excused.' [20]And another

---

Jesus then turns the lesson to the host. The Roman world ran on the patronage system, in which the rich and influential would curry favor among their constituencies in return for support, respect, and fulfilled obligations. In such a society, a family holding a lavish banquet for notable dignitaries and lesser functionaries would be renowned for their generosity and would thereby garner a great deal of influence in their local area. Such would be their payback.

The true act of generosity in the eyes of God, however, lies in bestowing respect and dignity on those who would not only be unable to repay in kind but whose very social standing carries no prestige whatsoever. The reward one gains in the resurrection of the righteous (Greek: *dikaios*) ties this lesson to the one Jesus teaches to the guests (v.14). In both instances, then, humility before God becomes the proper comportment for entering the kingdom.

14:15-24 The parable of the great banquet

This parable originates in Q and has a parallel in Matthew (22:1-14).

Banquets in the Gospel tradition always contain a strong eschatological element. Luke's creativity shines in this passage as he situates the banquet parable within the setting of a large dinner and gracefully folds the parable into the scene with the guest's remark in verse 15. The excuses that the original invitees give for not going to the dinner are legitimate. A wedding feast would last for several days, and one who has purchased land or cattle would have a strong desire to examine the sources of his livelihood. But these mitigating circumstances arise after they have presumably already accepted the invitation; it is the summons to enter the feast that they refuse. In a society in which a patronage system governs many areas of life, their refusals are a disrespectful insult to the host's generosity.

said, 'I have just married a woman, and therefore I cannot come.' ²¹The servant went and reported this to his master. Then the master of the house in a rage commanded his servant, 'Go out quickly into the streets and alleys of the town and bring in here the poor and the crippled, the blind and the lame.' ²²The servant reported, 'Sir, your orders have been carried out and still there is room.' ²³The master then ordered the servant, 'Go out to the highways and hedgerows and make people come in that my home may be filled. ²⁴For, I tell you, none of those men who were invited will taste my dinner.'"

Sayings on Discipleship. ²⁵Great crowds were traveling with him, and

---

Moreover, the last excuses introduce an eschatological dimension. According to Deuteronomic law, those who have built a house, planted a vineyard, or married a woman did not have to go on a military expedition or engage in any public duty for a period of one year (Deut 20:5-6; 24:5). By using these exemptions to explain why they cannot attend, they call attention to the dinner. The *eschaton* will not arrive without struggle. In order to sit at the banquet table in the kingdom of heaven, one must value it above any other facet of life, and acting on this value will be a struggle of warlike proportions. The banquet therefore becomes a metaphor for victory in the battle on behalf of the kingdom of God. Those refusing to come to the dinner demonstrate that they recognize this point. They simply do not hold the kingdom in as high regard as their daily affairs, as noble as those affairs may be.

The metaphor continues. The rich and wealthy have no need to participate in a banquet. The poor in the nearby city and district, who need the protection and favor of a rich lord, jump at the chance to go. There is still room at the table, so the invitation goes out to those who have no relationship to the host, and thus neither the host nor these guests have anything to gain from each other. The invitation is a purely gracious act.

The lesson of the parable places Jesus' mission in a microcosm. The self-satisfied, self-sufficient, and self-righteous are welcomed into the kingdom, but their self-inflated importance will block their will to enter. Those knowing their spiritual destitution will enter the kingdom willingly, and the Gentiles, who have no legal claim or right to come and dine, will also be invited to fill the dining hall.

14:25-35 The cost of discipleship

The Gospel of Matthew (10:37-38) shows a shortened parallel of verses 25-27. At the core of both accounts is Q source material, which Luke ex-

he turned and addressed them, [26]"If any one comes to me without hating his father and mother, wife and children, brothers and sisters, and even his own life, he cannot be my disciple. [27]Whoever does not carry his own cross and come after me cannot be my disciple. [28]Which of you wishing to construct a tower does not first sit down and calculate the cost to see if there is enough for its completion? [29]Otherwise, after laying the foundation and finding himself unable to finish the work the onlookers should laugh at him [30]and say, 'This one began to build but did not have the resources to finish.' [31]Or what king marching into battle would not first sit down and decide whether with ten thousand troops he can successfully oppose another king advancing upon him with twenty thousand troops? [32]But if not, while he

pands. The expansion continues into verses 28-33, a section that has no parallels. Luke concludes with a form of the saying about salt (vv. 34-35), which appears in all three Synoptics.

The language in verse 26 is harsh. In a reflection of the Semitic convention to employ hyperbole in order to make a point, Luke uses the Greek verb *miseō*, a term meaning "detest" or "abhor." The lesson teaches that no earthly attachment to a person, place, or thing should keep us from following God. Discipleship requires singleness of purpose, and this purpose is to go beyond natural ties and allegiances for the sake of the kingdom. Doing so will not be easy (v. 27).

The image seems to switch in verses 28-33, but the purpose of this scene is closely aligned to the preceding material and, in fact, explains it. Constructing a major building or preparing for a military expedition requires a great deal of planning. An architect or a general must calculate losses and the gains and make a decision accordingly. Being a disciple demands at least as much time and consideration. Disciples must acknowledge what they must sacrifice in order to take up the cross (v. 33).

References to building a tower and marching into battle may have been drawn from the life experience of the day. Herod the Great launched major construction in Caesarea Maritima, Jericho, Jerusalem, and even in the desert. Each of these projects involved a tremendous amount of planning to organize both human and material resources. Likewise, there was a major dispute between Herod Antipas and King Aretas of Nabatea, based on the former's divorce of his first wife, who was a Nabatean princess, in order to marry Herod Philip's wife, Herodias. Ultimately, this dispute turned into a war, which ended when Rome intervened and forced King Aretas to give up his plans.

is still far away, he will send a delegation to ask for peace terms. ³³In the same way, everyone of you who does not renounce all his possessions cannot be my disciple.

The Simile of Salt. ³⁴"Salt is good, but if salt itself loses its taste, with what can its flavor be restored? ³⁵It is fit neither for the soil nor for the manure pile; it is thrown out. Whoever has ears to hear ought to hear."

15 **The Parable of the Lost Sheep.** ¹The tax collectors and sinners were all drawing near to listen to him, ²but the Pharisees and scribes began to complain, saying, "This man welcomes sinners and eats with them." ³So to them he addressed this parable. ⁴"What

---

The whole lesson ends with the salt metaphor (vv. 34-35). In order for salt to lose its taste, it would have to cease being sodium chloride. Analogously, disciples who shrug off the cross cease being disciples of Christ.

15:1-32 Parables of the lost

At this point in the journey to Jerusalem, Luke has constructed a series of parables and lessons dealing with sinners and their chance for salvation.

Luke groups together three parables dealing with valuables lost and found. These parables form a unit in which the central personage in each story line is the Christ figure, and the person or object lost is then seen as the sinner. Two of the parables, those of the lost coin and the prodigal son, are found only in Luke's Gospel.

15:1-7 The parable of the lost sheep

Although this parable is Q material, Luke's introduction to it is different from Matthew 18:12-14. In Luke, Pharisees and scribes are grumbling about the tax collectors and sinners who gravitate toward Jesus. Their complaining leads into the parable of the lost sheep. The rhetorical question "What man among you . . . ?" (v. 4) relies on the common sense of the listener to conclude that no one would leave a whole flock to go after one lost sheep. The ridiculousness of leaving ninety-nine sheep in the desert to find a stray defies the imagination, but such ridiculousness is the point of the parable. Nearly equally ridiculous is inviting neighbors and friends to celebrate the return of the stray.

God's love for his creatures is so strong that it includes even the sinners, something that self-righteous individuals have a hard time appreciating. The joy that spreads through heaven also strikes our human ears as overmuch, but it emphasizes the divine welcome given to the repentant sinner.

The Greek uses *anthrōpos* for "man" (v. 4) and thus is a gender-inclusive term. Often in the Holy Land, both in antiquity and now, shepherds are

A market scene in Jerusalem

man among you having a hundred sheep and losing one of them would not leave the ninety-nine in the desert and go after the lost one until he finds it? ⁵And when he does find it, he sets it on his shoulders with great joy ⁶and, upon his arrival home, he calls together his friends and neighbors and says to them, 'Rejoice with me because I have found my lost sheep.' ⁷I tell you, in just the same way there will be more joy in heaven over one sinner who repents than over ninety-nine righteous people who have no need of repentance.

The Parable of the Lost Coin. ⁸"Or what woman having ten coins and losing one would not light a lamp and sweep the house, searching carefully until she finds it? ⁹And when she does find it, she calls together her friends and neighbors and says to them, 'Rejoice with me because I have found the coin that I lost.' ¹⁰In just the same way, I tell you, there will be rejoicing among

---

boys, girls, and women, an interesting perspective for the story considering that the shepherd is the Christ figure.

15:8-10 The parable of the lost coin

The Greek for "coin," *drachma*, was of the approximate value of a *denarius* and was worth about one day's wage for a laborer; the woman's diligent search, therefore, is certainly justified. When the object of the search, in this case a coin, is compared to the lost sheep in the previous parable, we can see an increase in the stakes. No matter how valuable one sheep is in earthly terms, it is not worth risking ninety-nine other sheep to find it. In this parable, however, the other nine coins are not placed in jeopardy as the woman seeks out the lost coin.

As with the parable of the yeast (13:20-21), the woman is the Christ figure, and her intense desire to find the lost coin is analogous to God's desire to find the lost sinner. Moreover, the parable says something about the value of the lost sinner in God's eyes. Here the mention of the rejoicing among the angels (v. 10) echoes the heavenly rejoicing found in the parable of the lost sheep (15:7). In both cases, such a conclusion keeps the eschatological focus of the message.

We read that a woman lights a lamp to sweep the house, a detail that gives evidence of the Syrian origins of Luke's Gospel. Unlike houses in the Judean Hills or even the semi-arid desert fringes of the south, which were constructed of comparatively lightweight limestone or sandstone, allowing for use of windows and other openings, houses on the Syrian plains and heights had a different building material and style altogether. In these areas the common building block was the very heavy, volcanic, black basalt stone. To support upper stories, the walls of these buildings

the angels of God over one sinner who repents."

The Parable of the Lost Son. [11]Then he said, "A man had two sons, [12]and the younger son said to his father, 'Father, give me the share of your estate that should come to me.' So the father divided the property between them. [13]After a few days, the younger son collected all his belongings and set off to a distant country where he squandered his inheritance on a life of dissipation.

[14]When he had freely spent everything, a severe famine struck that country, and he found himself in dire need. [15]So he hired himself out to one of the local citizens who sent him to his farm to tend the swine. [16]And he longed to eat his fill of the pods on which the swine fed, but nobody gave him any. [17]Coming to his senses he thought, 'How many of my father's hired workers have more than enough food to eat, but here am I, dying from hunger. [18]I shall get up and go to

had to be of solid construction and could not contain many, if any, windows. Consequently, interior living spaces were dark, and lighting a lamp would have been necessary, even in broad daylight.

15:11-32 The parable of the prodigal son

This parable has had a great influence on Western art, being depicted in drama, music, ballet, and painting.

The story opens with the younger son asking his father for his share of the inheritance. Of course, it is for the father to decide whether his son deserves it, not the son himself. By his action the younger son communicates that he does not view the inheritance as a gift bequeathed to him because of his father's good graces; rather, he sees it as his due.

According to ancient Jewish custom (Num 27:8-11; 36:7-9), an inheritance is the father's property, which, according to the custom of the day, the father gave to his sons, although he was not bound by any means to do so. When the younger son demands his share of the inheritance, therefore, he is asking the father for a part of the father's life. It is as if the son is requesting the father's very soul, an understanding emphasized by the Greek term for "property," *bios,* the same word used for "life" or "living" (v. 12). By his request, the son is indirectly demanding the father's own death. The father, however, instead of taking insult with his son's effrontery, gives him the inheritance.

The young son squanders the inheritance on "a life of dissipation" (v.13). The idea is that the son's living is so extravagant, profligate, wasteful, and glitzy, that there is nothing of merit in any of it. Not only is the son jeopardizing his physical life by dangerous living, but the return of enjoyment on his investment is so meager that it makes the whole venture worthless.

my father and I shall say to him, "Father, I have sinned against heaven and against you. ¹⁹I no longer deserve to be called your son; treat me as you would treat one of your hired workers."' ²⁰So he got up and went back to his father. While he was still a long way off, his father caught sight of him, and was filled with compassion. He ran to his son, embraced him and kissed him.

²¹His son said to him, 'Father, I have sinned against heaven and against you; I no longer deserve to be called your son.' ²²But his father ordered his servants, 'Quickly bring the finest robe and put it on him; put a ring on his finger and sandals on his feet. ²³Take the fattened calf and slaughter it. Then let us celebrate with a feast, ²⁴because this son of mine was dead, and has come to

---

To feed a pig, which represents everything reprehensible to every Jewish sensibility, would be a curse indeed. God-fearing Gentiles in the Lukan community would have been familiar enough with Jewish customs to know how low the young son descended. The son is absolutely alienated from the community. The pods (Greek: *kerátion*) were probably from the carob tree and would be fit for human consumption (v. 16).

With verse 17 the audience is prepared for the next part, where the son acknowledges his sinfulness: "Father, I have sinned against heaven and against you; I no longer deserve to be called your son" (vv. 18b-19). Despite his egregiously bad behavior, he plans to ask for the status of a hired hand, which actually is how his father should have and could have treated him when he asked for the inheritance in the first place.

Father and son meet in verse 20, and the son begins his rehearsed speech, but he does not get to finish it. The father, so moved and filled with emotion at his son's return, does not hear a word he says. He cuts the son off in mid-sentence and tells the servants to prepare for a party, and he explains, "because this son of mine was dead, and has come to life again; he was lost and has been found" (v. 24). Because the son never has the opportunity to call himself a "hired hand," one cannot say that the father is refuting his son's assessment. Rather, we the audience can see that the father has always held this son in high regard and has never stopped loving him. The father's love and generosity toward his lost, now found son so border on the ridiculous that his actions preclude his wayward son's expression of shame and guilt. We have here a loving father whose love exceeds all bounds.

This parable then switches focus to the elder brother (v. 25). By external measure, the elder brother has been obedient and respectful of the father, whom his younger brother has both insulted and grieved. The dialogue

life again; he was lost, and has been found.' Then the celebration began. ²⁵Now the older son had been out in the field and, on his way back, as he neared the house, he heard the sound of music and dancing. ²⁶He called one of the servants and asked what this might mean. ²⁷The servant said to him, 'Your brother has returned and your father has slaughtered the fattened calf because he has him back safe and sound.' ²⁸He became angry, and when he refused to enter the house, his father came out and pleaded with him. ²⁹He said to his father in reply, 'Look, all these years I served you and not once did I disobey your orders; yet you never gave me even a young goat to feast on with my friends. ³⁰But when your son returns who swallowed up your property with prostitutes, for him you slaughter the fattened calf.' ³¹He said to him, 'My son, you are here with me always; everything I have is yours. ³²But now we must celebrate and rejoice, because your brother was dead and has come to life again; he was lost and has been found.'"

---

between the son and the father, however, challenges such an assumption of his filial relationship.

The elder brother, after citing off his own virtues, explodes in front of his father (v. 29-30). The father, defending his own act of forgiveness, corrects the elder brother (v. 32). The father insists that the prodigal son is both a son to him and a brother to his other son. The one who has been alienated is now restored to the family.

The elder son is blind to his father's magnanimity. As an elder son, he has a duty to support the father in his decisions, a duty that he obviously shirks. The positions are reversed. Now it is the elder brother who insults and acts disrespectfully, while the younger son, by humbling himself, shows respect. In spite of this, the father still goes on loving, this time toward the elder son (v. 31). The father's forgiveness and charity maintain the ties of a loving relationship toward both his sons. As with all parables, this one turns to the listener, asking us to identify with either the younger son, the elder brother, or the father.

In each of the successive parables of the lost, that which is lost increases in value, from stray lamb, to a drachma, to a son. With such a progression, the worth of the sinner also increases in God's eyes, and the listener is left with the conclusion that God loves all as parents love their children. Furthermore, in the first two parables the shepherd and the woman are the Christ figure, respectively. In the parable of the prodigal son, however, it is not absolutely clear whether the father is Christ or God the Father, and this ambiguity, no doubt, is intentional.

16 The Parable of the Dishonest Steward.

¹Then he also said to his disciples, "A rich man had a steward who was reported to him for squandering his property. ²He summoned him and said, 'What is this I hear about you? Prepare a full account of your stewardship, because you can no longer be my steward.' ³The steward said to himself, 'What shall I do, now that my master is taking the position of steward away from me? I am not strong enough to dig and I am ashamed to beg. ⁴I know what I shall do so that, when I am removed from the stewardship, they may welcome me into their homes.' ⁵He called in his master's debtors one by one. To the first he said, 'How much do you owe my master?' ⁶He replied, 'One hundred measures of olive oil.' He said to him, 'Here is your promissory note. Sit down and quickly write one for fifty.' ⁷Then to another he said, 'And you, how much do you owe?' He replied, 'One hundred kors of wheat.' He said to him, 'Here is your promissory note; write one for eighty.' ⁸And the master commended that dishonest steward for acting prudently.

Application of the Parable. "For the children of this world are more prudent in dealing with their own generation than are the children of light. ⁹I tell you, make friends for yourselves with dishonest wealth, so that when it fails, you will be welcomed into eternal dwellings. ¹⁰The person who is trustworthy in very small matters is also

---

16:1-13 The parable of the dishonest steward

This parable appears only in Luke's Gospel. That the steward is clever to the point of being crafty makes the fact that Jesus commends him difficult for us to appreciate.

Stewards made a living by collecting rents and debts for their masters and charging the debtors interest on the amount owed, which would then go to the stewards' coffers. Here the steward is shameless in the lengths he will go to maintain his position. He is not trying to hide anything from the rich man; indeed, he may even want his employer to find out about his altering the books. His hope is that his cleverness may win back the rich man's favor, and barring that outcome, he will at least have made some grateful constituents to take him in. The steward's audaciousness in achieving his ends calls attention to Jesus' lesson. Anyone of us would go to the greatest lengths, no matter how unsavory, to ensure a secure place in this world; how much more should we devote our attention to the world to come (v.8).

Jesus names the problem in verse 9. The term "dishonest wealth" reflects the danger that inheres in worldly goods. Jesus warns the listener to use the wealth, but not to place any trust in it. Only trusting in God will lead to an eternal dwelling; everything else is counterfeit.

trustworthy in great ones; and the person who is dishonest in very small matters is also dishonest in great ones. [11]If, therefore, you are not trustworthy with dishonest wealth, who will trust you with true wealth? [12]If you are not trustworthy with what belongs to another, who will give you what is yours? [13]No servant can serve two masters. He will either hate one and love the other, or be devoted to one and despise the other. You cannot serve God and mammon."

A Saying against the Pharisees. [14]The Pharisees, who loved money, heard all these things and sneered at him. [15]And he said to them, "You justify yourselves in the sight of others, but God knows your hearts; for what is of human esteem is an abomination in the sight of God.

Sayings about the Law. [16]"The law and the prophets lasted until John; but from then on the kingdom of God is proclaimed, and everyone who enters

---

The narrative then discusses the conclusions one can draw from the parable by indirectly referring to the description of the steward (vv. 10-13). In verse 1 the steward is accused of "squandering" the master's property. The steward has mismanaged, perhaps through incompetence, the "very small matters" of this world, so there is no reason to trust him in the larger matters of the next one (v. 10). That lesson is turned toward the audience in verse 12. Trust is earned, it is not assumed. Those who deal loosely and unethically with others should not expect others to honor and trust them.

Verse 13 is a Q saying that also appears in Matthew 6:24. "Mammon" (v. 13), a Greek transliteration of the Aramaic word, means more than wealth and riches; it can signify anything of this world that one relies on: titles, positions, privileges, and honors. To be sure, wealth is tied up with many of these perquisites, but mammon is anything which takes our attention away from God, the true source of life.

16:14-15 Encounter with the Pharisees

Luke alone features this reproof, which, with the notice that this particular group of Pharisees "loved money" (v. 14), is tied to the warning about wealth above. Jesus directs the criticism at the human desire for self-justification and public praise. The performance of good deeds, then, goes only as far as human acclaim. In such a case, people will never do an act that may be good but unpopular.

16:16-18 Sayings on the Law and divorce

The "law" in this passage refers to the Mosaic Law, the Jewish religious and cultic legislation, and reflects the context from which the Christian movement emerged. The evangelists and other New Testament

does so with violence. [17]It is easier for heaven and earth to pass away than for the smallest part of a letter of the law to become invalid.

Sayings about Divorce. [18]"Everyone who divorces his wife and marries another commits adultery, and the one who marries a woman divorced from her husband commits adultery.

The Parable of the Rich Man and Lazarus. [19]"There was a rich man who dressed in purple garments and fine linen and dined sumptuously each day. [20]And lying at his door was a poor man named Lazarus, covered with sores, [21]who would gladly have eaten his fill of the scraps that fell from the rich man's table. Dogs even used to come

---

writers interpreted the Old Testament, comprised of books both in Hebrew and Greek, as the precursor to the revelation of Christ. Now the "kingdom of God is proclaimed," but the ability to move into a new way of viewing one's relationship with God is not easy; hence "everyone who enters does so with violence" (v. 16). Jewish Christians found that the change from the Mosaic Law to Christ required a major shift in focus, and Gentile Christians, at first not welcome unless they had undergone conversion to Judaism (see Acts 10; 15), put themselves at risk with their pagan neighbors. Luke's Gospel stresses Christ as the ultimate arbiter of any interpretation of the Law (v. 17); in that sense, the law will not pass away, as the next saying demonstrates (v. 18).

Luke and Mark agree against Matthew in their readings on the prohibition of divorce. While Matthew sees unchastity as a mitigating circumstance for dissolving the marriage (see Matt 19:9; Mark 10:11-12), Luke's version of divorce legislation (v. 18) serves as an example of how the Law has lost its validity. According to the Mosaic teaching, a man could divorce his wife by simply signing a statement of dismissal; the woman had no similar option (Deut 24:1-4). Consequently, the woman and her children would be left to fend for themselves by begging and prostitution. Jesus nullifies this legislation by declaring that no one can divorce, and thereby demonstrates that the law and the prophets ended with John (v. 16).

16:19-31 The rich man and Lazarus

This parable appears only in Luke and reflects the evangelist's overriding concern for the poor and for social justice. In the tradition this is also known as the story of Dives and Lazarus, the former name stemming from the Latin *dives*, meaning "rich person." It is one of the best known of all Gospel stories, even prompting Ralph Vaughan Williams to compose a musical score based on this story. The name "Lazarus" itself is the Greek transliteration of the Hebrew abbreviation "Eleazar," a name that means

and lick his sores. ²²When the poor man died, he was carried away by angels to the bosom of Abraham. The rich man also died and was buried, ²³and from the netherworld, where he was in torment, he raised his eyes and saw Abraham far off and Lazarus at his side. ²⁴And he cried out, 'Father Abraham, have pity on me. Send Lazarus to dip the tip of his finger in water and cool my tongue, for I am suffering torment in these flames.' ²⁵Abraham replied, 'My child, remember that you received what was good during your lifetime while Lazarus likewise received what was bad; but now he is comforted here, whereas you are tormented. ²⁶Moreover, between us and you a great chasm is established to prevent anyone from crossing who might wish to go from our side to yours or from your side to ours.' ²⁷He said, 'Then I beg you, father, send

"God has helped." Thematically, it is tied to the saying about God and mammon in 16:13.

The information concerning the rich man's clothing (v. 19) indicates that he is not simply well off—he is excessively wealthy. Purple dye was a costly commodity that very few people even among the rich could afford. These details heighten the contrast between the rich man and Lazarus, who not only has sores that dogs would lick but who even lacks the simplest garment to cover those sores. That Lazarus keeps company with dogs accentuates his dismal state, since dogs were considered filthy, undesirable animals.

Luke illustrates the theme of the great reversal in this parable, first outlined in the *Magnificat* (see Luke 1:46-55). In the parable the hungry are literally "filled with good things," while the rich are "sent away empty" (1:53). The dialogue between Abraham and the rich man amply describes the new state of things. We know that the rich man cannot claim ignorance of the fact that someone hungry is outside his door, for he refers to Lazarus by name (v. 24). There is even an arrogant tone in his request: he does not ask Abraham for the favor but requests that Abraham command Lazarus to come down and refresh him. Most likely he treated Lazarus in a similar fashion when they both were alive.

Abraham, in his reply, ensures that the rich man knows exactly why he is where he is so that neither the rich man, now suffering the flames of the netherworld, nor the audience can conclude that he is a victim of a great misfortune. No, the rich man's lack of charity and responsibility put him there; indeed, the rich man's great sin of omission fashioned the chasm between the two. We are forced to wonder why the chasm cannot be crossed. The answer says a great deal about salvation and damnation.

him to my father's house, [28]for I have five brothers, so that he may warn them, lest they too come to this place of torment.' [29]But Abraham replied, 'They have Moses and the prophets. Let them listen to them.' [30]He said, 'Oh no, father Abraham, but if someone from the dead goes to them, they will repent.' [31]Then Abraham said, 'If they will not listen to Moses and the prophets, neither will they be persuaded if someone should rise from the dead.'"

17 Temptations to Sin. [1]He said to his disciples, "Things that cause sin will inevitably occur, but woe to the person through whom they occur. [2]It would be better for him if a millstone were put around his neck and he be thrown into the sea than for him to cause one of these little ones to sin. [3]Be ▶

The lesson is not that God is a God of damnation and punishment, inasmuch as it gives us an example of how much of a role we play in our salvation. The rich man was oblivious to the needs of those around him while he was alive, and now that he is dead, he is still oblivious, as his call for Lazarus's services suggests. Herein lies the danger of wealth that Jesus always preaches: power and wealth blind us to the kingdom of God in this life and in the next. If we are not wide-eyed to the kingdom and its demands now, as Moses and the prophets tell us to be (v. 31), we will not be sensitive to seeing the kingdom after we die. The great irony in the story is that the rich man needs Lazarus in order to be saved. Had he paid attention to Lazarus begging for table scraps at the door of his house, the rich man would not be in the predicament he is in now.

The last verse of the parable, of course, is a reference to Jesus' own resurrection.

17:1-4 Temptations to sin

The journey to Jerusalem continues with further instruction along the way.

Each Synoptic Gospel has a variation of the warning against giving offense. Verses 3-4 parallel Matthew 18:15, thereby making them Q material. Luke injects a note of reality in verse 1b: as long as there is a believing community, there will be scandals. As great a sin as it is to lead one into temptation, it is far greater to do so to a "little one" (v. 2). Millstones, even one for household use, were heavy and expensive. The punishment suggested is severe indeed.

Where there is sin, there must be forgiveness, and Luke gracefully connects the two. We have another example of the mercy and tenderness that are so much a part of the Third Gospel. This mercy and tenderness, however, are not to be regarded as permission for further injury. Those who

on your guard! If your brother sins, rebuke him; and if he repents, forgive him. ⁴And if he wrongs you seven times in one day and returns to you seven times saying, 'I am sorry,' you should forgive him."

Saying of Faith. ⁵And the apostles said to the Lord, "Increase our faith." ⁶The Lord replied, "If you have faith the size of a mustard seed, you would say to [this] mulberry tree, 'Be up-rooted and planted in the sea,' and it would obey you.

Attitude of a Servant. ⁷"Who among you would say to your servant who has just come in from plowing or tending sheep in the field, 'Come here immediately and take your place at table'? ⁸Would he not rather say to him, 'Prepare something for me to eat. Put on your apron and wait on me while I eat and drink. You may eat and drink

---

sin are to be rebuked, and if sinners repent, they are to be forgiven. The Gospel sees rebuke and forgiveness as a means of achieving both personal salvation and social justice. On the other hand, lest repentance and forgiveness be exercised on a quid pro quo basis, the saying continues with the proviso that because sins or even the same sin will occur numerous times, it must be forgiven each time the sinner repents. We are to imitate divine forgiveness in its limitlessness.

This passage addresses only how to deal with sinful behavior within the church community, but for Luke, mercy extends to those outside the community as well (see Luke 6:27-36).

17:5-6 Saying on faith

Once again, faith is compared to a mustard seed (see Luke 13:19), but the example switches to a sycamine tree (*morus nigra*; read "mulberry" in the text), a large tree with clustered berries. Both Matthew and Luke use the hyperbole from Q to make their point that nothing is impossible to the person who has faith. Matthew's phrase, however, refers to moving a mountain, which most scholars believe to be the original version.

17:7-10 The attitude of a servant

This piece on servants occurs only in Luke.

The social world of the Gospel is particularly evident in this passage dealing with masters and slaves. The lesson is that Christians should not expect praise and honor for performing those duties that they are obligated to perform. Moreover, the saying counters the thought that salvation can be gained on human merit alone and without God's grace. If our own deeds render us unprofitable servants, we have no other recourse for salvation than to depend on the divine initiative.

when I am finished'? ⁹Is he grateful to that servant because he did what was commanded? ¹⁰So should it be with you. When you have done all you have been commanded, say, 'We are unprofitable servants; we have done what we were obliged to do.'"

The Cleansing of Ten Lepers. ¹¹As he continued his journey to Jerusalem, he traveled through Samaria and Galilee. ¹²As he was entering a village, ten lepers met [him]. They stood at a distance from him ¹³and raised their voice, saying, "Jesus, Master! Have pity on us!" ¹⁴And when he saw them, he said, "Go show yourselves to the priests." As they were going they were cleansed. ¹⁵And one of them, realizing he had been healed, returned, glorifying God in a loud voice; ¹⁶and he fell at the feet of Jesus and thanked him. He was a Samaritan. ¹⁷Jesus said in reply, "Ten were cleansed, were they not? Where are the other nine? ¹⁸Has none but this foreigner returned to give thanks to God?" ¹⁹Then he said to him, "Stand up and go; your faith has saved you."

The Coming of the Kingdom of God. ²⁰Asked by the Pharisees when the kingdom of God would come, he said in reply, "The coming of the kingdom of God cannot be observed, ²¹and

17:11-19 The cleansing of ten lepers

The prescription to the lepers to show themselves to the priests is found in Leviticus 14:2-9.

The most common route for Jews in Galilee to go to Jerusalem was through the Jordan Valley. Although cutting down through Samaria was not impossible, most Jews preferred to avoid Samaritan territory (see Luke 9:52). Did Jesus ever set foot in Samaria? Verse 11 can be translated "through the region between Samaria and Galilee." This passage is solely Lukan material and shows Luke's proclivity to highlight the faith of the social outcast over that of the established insider. Both Jews (Galileans) and Samaritans compose this group of lepers; both are society's outcasts, and therefore they associate with each other.

Luke's eschatological vision comes into focus with the emphasis on faith in verse 19. Jesus instructs the Samaritan leper, not that his faith has cured him, but that his faith has "saved" him. The leper is not only saved from his leprosy but gains eternal salvation—all from faith. The connection of faith with salvation occurs throughout Luke's Gospel, as we have seen with the woman in the house of Simon the Pharisee (7:50), the cure of the hemorrhaging woman (8:48), and even at the cross (23:43).

17:20-37 The coming of the kingdom and the Son of Man

In verses 20-21 Luke expresses a realized eschatology that supports the vision displayed in the dialogue with the Samaritan leper above.

no one will announce, 'Look, here it is,' or, 'There it is.' For behold, the kingdom of God is among you."

The Day of the Son of Man. ²²Then he said to his disciples, "The days will come when you will long to see one of the days of the Son of Man, but you will not see it. ²³There will be those who will say to you, 'Look, there he is,' [or] 'Look, here he is.' Do not go off, do not run in pursuit. ²⁴For just as lightning flashes and lights up the sky from one side to the other, so will the Son of Man be [in his day]. ²⁵But first he must suffer greatly and be rejected by this generation. ²⁶As it was in the days of Noah, so it will be in the days of the Son of Man; ²⁷they were eating and drinking, marrying and giving in marriage up to the day that Noah entered the ark, and the flood

---

Indeed, the last phrase in verse 21 seems Johannine in its language as it underscores an *eschaton* already present.

The tone and theme switch suddenly to a future-oriented eschatology in verse 22. The opening words of this verse in Greek, which the English translation expresses, indicate a reversal of thought. In this first encounter with Lukan apocalyptic writing, the reading draws a parallel between sudden acts of destruction in the Old Testament and the Son of Man's impending arrival on the earth. Although found far more often in Ezekiel than in Daniel, the latter's use of "Son of Man" has greater bearing on the synoptic understanding of this term, an understanding that Luke shares. The heavily apocalyptic material in Daniel (see Dan 7:13; 8:15-17) is reflected in verse 22 and also figures prominently in the book of Revelation.

Luke includes a warning about following false prophets (as do the parallels in Mark and Matthew), but he also connects the coming of the *eschaton* with the fate awaiting Jesus in Jerusalem (v. 25). Furthermore, Luke builds a sense of urgency by relating Lot's escape from the explosive conflagration that destroyed Sodom; people should be vigilant and anxious. This sense of urgency also has a social justice theme, for injustice and oppression were the reasons for Sodom's obliteration (see Isa 1:9-16; Ezek 16:49-52). Any desire to hold on to the present is discouraged, and Lot's wife stands as an example of what might happen to the one who tarries. Those who make no permanent claims to this life will always be ready for the *eschaton* (v. 31).

To separate Jesus' words from the Gospel writer's is always extremely difficult. In this passage it is impossible. Verse 31 appears to be a prediction after the fact. Josephus describes the sudden arrival of the Romans at the gates of Jerusalem during the First Jewish Revolt (A.D. 66–70; *J.W.* 5.2.3]. Few if any were able to escape the destruction and massacre. The early Christians most likely interpreted the Jewish rebellion and the

came and destroyed them all. ²⁸Similarly, as it was in the days of Lot: they were eating, drinking, buying, selling, planting, building; ²⁹on the day when Lot left Sodom, fire and brimstone rained from the sky to destroy them all. ³⁰So it will be on the day the Son of Man is revealed. ³¹On that day, a person who is on the housetop and whose belongings are in the house must not go down to get them, and likewise a person in the field must not return to what was left behind. ³²Remember the wife of Lot. ³³Whoever seeks to preserve his life will lose it, but whoever loses it will save it.

³⁴I tell you, on that night there will be two people in one bed; one will be taken, the other left. ³⁵And there will be two women grinding meal together; one will be taken, the other left." ³⁶ ³⁷They said to him in reply, "Where, Lord?" He said to them, "Where the body is, there also the vultures will gather."

18 **The Parable of the Persistent Widow.** ¹Then he told them a parable about the necessity for them to pray always without becoming weary. He said, ²"There was a judge in a certain town who neither feared God nor respected any human being. ³And a

destruction of Jerusalem with its splendid temple as the fulfillment of Jesus' words, even as those words were mixed into their experiences of the catastrophe. What we have here is an amalgam of Q material, oral tradition, memory, and Lukan editing. (See Luke 21:20-24.)

One cannot take every passage of Scripture literally and apart from a larger theological context. Nowhere is this truer than in apocalyptic literature. Readers should be on guard against determining the saved, the damned, and the rapture by reading this material. Verse 37, in encouraging us to read the signs of the times, advises us to keep the whole Christian tradition in focus as we interpret those signs. And what are the signs? Jesus does not say, and this point is the essential part of the apocalyptic message.

Christians are to concern themselves with doing the will of God, for which Jesus has given his disciples abundant examples: taking care of the poor, trusting in God alone, and forgiving enemies. We are not to waste time trying to predict the future. The paradoxical presentation of the kingdom as already present (v. 21) and not yet here (v. 30) expresses its true reality. The kingdom will be manifested in living the life of Christ.

18:1-8 The parable of the persistent widow

Situating this pericope after the apocalyptic passage regarding the Son of Man offers the believer the proper way to maintain vigilance for the parousia, or second coming. With prayer and praying mentioned over thirty times in Luke's Gospel and the Acts of the Apostles, the parable of the persistent widow highlights this central feature of Luke's Gospel by

widow in that town used to come to him and say, 'Render a just decision for me against my adversary.' ⁴For a long time the judge was unwilling, but eventually he thought, 'While it is true that I neither fear God nor respect any human being, ⁵because this widow keeps bothering me I shall deliver a just decision for her lest she finally come and strike me.'" ⁶The Lord said, "Pay attention to what the dishonest judge says. ⁷Will not God then secure the rights of his chosen ones who call out to him day and night? Will he be slow to answer them? ⁸I tell you, he will see to it that justice is done for them speedily. But when the Son of Man comes, will he find faith on earth?"

The Parable of the Pharisee and the Tax Collector. ⁹He then addressed this parable to those who were convinced of their own righteousness and despised everyone else. ¹⁰"Two people went up to the temple area to pray; one

emphasizing the necessity and efficacy of constant prayer. Moreover, because widows and orphans were to be special recipients of charity according to Jewish law (Deut 24:17-22), the early Christians would have been particularly attentive to the teaching.

The story appears only in Luke, and there are at least two ways to read it. The first is to see the unjust judge as the protagonist bearing the lesson for the reader. Similar to the literary style found in the parable of the dishonest steward (16:1-8), the intent of the teaching comes through the comparison of the greater: As an unjust judge grants a petition solely for self-serving purposes, how much more will a loving God grant the desires of his beloved petitioner.

A second, feminist interpretation, on the other hand, sees the widow as the protagonist and thus the vehicle for the lesson. In this case, she, in her weakness, becomes the Christ figure who combats evil and injustice on behalf of the poor and neglected. She is unstinting in her efforts, and the unjust judge, the symbol of oppression, is clearly afraid of her, as seen from the Greek verb *hypōpiazō* for "strike" (v. 5), which means to "treat roughly, maltreat, strike under the eye." Here, too, the intent of the teaching surfaces through analogy: As persistent as a widow is to secure her rights, so is God in securing the rights of those petitioning him.

The reference to the Son of Man (v. 8) brings the parable in line with the teaching on the last days (17:22-37): Pray constantly while living and working for the kingdom of God.

18:9-14 The parable of the Pharisee and the tax collector

This parable, also found only in Luke, continues the theme on prayer. Whereas the parable of the persistent widow (18:1-8) shows the necessity

was a Pharisee and the other was a tax collector. ¹¹The Pharisee took up his position and spoke this prayer to himself, 'O God, I thank you that I am not like the rest of humanity—greedy, dishonest, adulterous—or even like this tax collector. ¹²I fast twice a week, and I pay tithes on my whole income.' ¹³But the tax collector stood off at a distance and would not even raise his eyes to heaven but beat his breast and prayed, 'O God, be merciful to me a sinner.' ¹⁴I tell you, the latter went home justified, not the former; for everyone who exalts himself will be humbled, and the one who humbles himself will be exalted."

Saying on Children and the Kingdom. ¹⁵People were bringing even infants to him that he might touch them, and when the disciples saw this, they

---

of constant prayer, the parable of the Pharisee and the tax collector displays the proper comportment for prayer.

No doubt the Pharisee does everything he says he does. Fasting and tithing are not only good things to do, but the former is also proclaimed by the prophets while the latter is required by the Law (see Deut 14:22-29). The purpose of the parable is not to discourage religious and pious practice; rather, its function is to call into question the reasons why people take on devotional works. The Pharisee gives the reasons for deeds: they are to justify himself in the world's eyes as well as in the eyes of God. Luke underscores this point in verse 9.

In contrast, the tax collector does nothing pious that we know of. In fact, as a tax collector, it would be most surprising if he ever did anything good for anyone. During the Roman occupation, tax collectors were not only traitors to their own people but also extortionists feeding off their compatriots. Furthermore, their dealing with the pagan Romans made them ritually impure, thereby excommunicating themselves from their fellow Jews. Compared with the dedicated, devoted Pharisee, a tax collector would never be considered honest, pious, or holy. Unlike the Pharisee, however, the tax collector knows his sinfulness. He pleads for mercy and demonstrates his need for God. The Pharisee, on the other hand, in singing his own praises, makes God his beneficiary. That the tax collector leaves justified was as shocking to the first-century audience as it is to us. So important is this parable that it sets the tone for those participating in the passion and crucifixion (see 23:48).

18:15-17 Access to the kingdom

This passage stresses that the people brought infants to Jesus, whereas the parallels in Mark and Matthew read only that children came. The mention of infants gives a glimpse of the sociological structure in the

rebuked them. [16]Jesus, however, called the children to himself and said, "Let the children come to me and do not prevent them; for the kingdom of God belongs to such as these. [17]Amen, I say to you, whoever does not accept the kingdom of God like a child will not enter it."

The Rich Official. [18]An official asked him this question, "Good teacher, what must I do to inherit eternal life?" [19]Jesus answered him, "Why do you call me good? No one is good but God alone. [20]You know the commandments, 'You shall not commit adultery; you shall not kill; you shall not steal; you shall not bear false witness; honor your father and your mother.'" [21]And he replied, "All of these I have observed from my youth." [22]When Jesus heard this he said to him, "There is still one thing left for you: sell all that you have and distribute it to the

---

ancient world. Conversions were never individualistic or isolated events. If the master or mistress of the household became a follower of Christ, everyone in the extended family and even the slaves did as well. In the Acts of the Apostles we read similar accounts regarding baptism (Acts 16:15, 33; 18:8). Luke's reading could very well reflect and suggest the practice of infant baptism in the early church.

Society today often presents Christianity as a childish, trivial, or trite matter and will use passages like this one to justify doing so. To "accept the kingdom of God like a child," however, means to receive the kingdom of God with an open guilelessness to the gift that God offers, something that requires a healthy maturity. In this case, the tax collector in the preceding passage (18:9-14) is the perfect example of open guilelessness.

18:18-23 The rich official

Although in their respective versions of the story, both Matthew and Mark simply state that a man comes up to Jesus, Luke specifies that the one asking the question is a ruler. Thus Luke informs the reader that the individual is not only rich but also powerful, an important point for the story.

The ruler's fault is one of complacency, and in this regard he is similar to the Pharisee in 18:9-14. When he calls Jesus "Good teacher" (v. 18), Jesus responds in a sharp tone, because he can see through the unctuous language. The ruler hopes that by flattery he can increase in stature to gain eternal life. Jesus continues with listing the prescriptions of the Decalogue. These statutes should recall the whole Exodus experience, in which the people struggle between their ever present faithlessness and their eventual trust in God. The ruler's answer that he has observed all the commandments from his youth demonstrates that he has completely forgotten that covenantal relationship expressed by trust in God.

119

poor, and you will have a treasure in heaven. Then come, follow me." ²³But when he heard this he became quite sad, for he was very rich.

On Riches and Renunciation. ²⁴Jesus looked at him [now sad] and said, "How hard it is for those who have wealth to enter the kingdom of God! ²⁵For it is easier for a camel to pass through the eye of a needle than for a rich person to enter the kingdom of God." ²⁶Those who heard this said, "Then who can be saved?" ²⁷And he said, "What is impossible for human beings is possible for God." ²⁸Then Peter said, "We have given up our possessions and followed you." ²⁹He said to them, "Amen, I say to you, there is no one who has given up house or wife or brothers or parents or children for

---

Jesus concludes by entering the ruler's mind-set. The first half of the answer would catch the man's attention, "There is still one thing left for you . . ." (v. 22a). The ruler can handle the challenge; by his wits he has already accumulated wealth and power. Then comes the surprise: "sell all that you have and distribute it to the poor . . . come follow me" (v. 22b). The man's sadness results from a double realization. The first is that he must surrender everything of worth in his life, and the second follows, namely, that everything he thought was of great value both in this life and the next is actually worthless. His life from his youth has been an act of faithlessness. To inherit eternal life, he must stop trusting in what he has trusted and place his trust in God.

18:24-30 On entering the kingdom of God

The dialogue with the rich official prompts Jesus' comment on the ease of a camel going through the eye of a needle, one of the most challenging verses in the Gospel (v. 25). The response from the crowd is certainly understandable: "Then who can be saved?" (v. 26).

A long-standing interpretation of this passage is that there was in Jerusalem a gate called the "Eye of the Needle," which required a cargo-laden camel to rest on all four legs and crawl through the door in order to enter the city. There is no evidence anywhere in the Mideast, however, of any gate called the "Eye of the Needle." In addition, camels are unable to crawl. Jesus is using a form of hyperbole that is a natural part of Semitic speech.

The lesson that arises from this encounter with the ruler is similar to the one taught in the parable of the dishonest steward (16:1-13), where trusting in one's own wealth and accomplishments instead of in God makes salvation difficult if not impossible. In both cases the responsibility for accepting salvation falls on us. Those who place all hope in their own accomplishments will never be open to God's mercy, simply because they

the sake of the kingdom of God ³⁰who will not receive [back] an overabundant return in this present age and eternal life in the age to come."

The Third Prediction of the Passion. ³¹Then he took the Twelve aside and said to them, "Behold, we are going up to Jerusalem and everything written by the prophets about the Son of Man will be fulfilled. ³²He will be handed over to the Gentiles and he will be mocked and insulted and spat upon; ³³and after they have scourged him they will kill him, but on the third day he will rise." ³⁴But they understood nothing of this; the word remained hidden from them and they failed to comprehend what he said.

The Healing of the Blind Beggar. ³⁵Now as he approached Jericho a blind

---

have let worldly values blind themselves to it. Since power and wealth are idols, and seductive ones at that, the ruler in the story and others like him cannot even see the way into the kingdom, let alone enter it. In this sense, it is easier for a camel to pass through a needle's eye.

Peter, sensing the meaning of Jesus' hyperbolic example, responds in verse 28. His statement implies that he is looking for an answer as to whether he and the other disciples are saved or not. Jesus does not answer directly; rather, his reply is addressed in the third person (vv. 29-30). Jesus' statement reflects a realized eschatology as well as a future one. Forsaking worldly comfort has a present reward, yet the reward is not fully realized until one reaches eternal life. Unlike the Markan parallel, which speaks of persecutions along with the rewards (Mark 10:30), Luke does not mention such hardships. Because the next passage contains the third prediction of the passion, Luke avoids the redundancy by not including the sobering fact here.

This passage has been used over the centuries as a rationale for religious life.

18:31-34 The third prediction of the passion

Being a disciple has its rewards, but it also has difficulties, as Jesus reminds his band of followers with this third, final, and most vivid prediction of his passion (see 9:22, 44-45; but also 17:25).

Although both Matthew and Mark feature parallels to this passage, only Luke contains information about the prophets (v. 31) and the Twelve's inability to understand what Jesus is saying (v. 34).

18:35-43 The blind beggar of Jericho

Jesus is relentlessly pursuing his intent as described in 9:51. In going from Galilee to Jerusalem through the Jordan Valley, one would turn west at Jericho in order to take the Wadi Qelt road up into the Judean moun-

man was sitting by the roadside begging, ³⁶and hearing a crowd going by, he inquired what was happening. ³⁷They told him, "Jesus of Nazareth is passing by." ³⁸He shouted, "Jesus, Son of David, have pity on me!" ³⁹The people walking in front rebuked him, telling him to be silent, but he kept calling out all the more, "Son of David, have pity on me!" ⁴⁰Then Jesus stopped and ordered that he be brought to him; and when he came near, Jesus asked him, ⁴¹"What do you want me to do for you?" He replied, "Lord, please let me see." ⁴²Jesus told him, "Have sight; your faith has saved you." ⁴³He immediately received his sight and followed him, giving glory to God. When they saw this, all the people gave praise to God.

19 **Zacchaeus the Tax Collector.** ¹He came to Jericho and intended to pass through the town. ²Now

tains. Jericho, an oasis and a prosperous city in Judea, was also the locale of Herod the Great's winter palace. These facts serve to accentuate the beggar's lowly social position.

All three synoptic accounts contain this story, but only Mark gives the blind man a name (Bartimaeus; see Mark 10:46). Comparisons are very important here. This blind man can "see" Jesus is the Messiah, whereas the Twelve cannot understand what he is saying (v. 34). This paradox fits well within the Gospel tradition, where the blind usually "see," while those who "see" are actually blind.

The beggar uses one of the earliest Christian titles applied to Christ, "Son of David" (v. 38), a title that rarely appears in Luke (see 3:31; 20:41). Jesus hears the distressful cry despite the commotion of the crowd and their efforts to silence the man. Jesus could have walked to the man, but he commands that the beggar be brought to him (v. 40). Among religious people of the time, physical disability was linked to sinfulness. By having the crowd lead the blind man to him, Jesus induces them to take responsibility for healing him, thereby redefining both suffering and sin. Jesus does not assume that the beggar wants to see; rather, he asks him to explicitly state his need (v. 41). Of course, the beggar requests sight, because he knows that Jesus can grant it, and by this action he demonstrates his faith. Hence Jesus can say, "Your faith has saved you" (v. 42). In true Lukan fashion, in the end everyone—beggar and crowd—glorifies God.

19:1-10 Zacchaeus the tax collector

This passage appears only in Luke and concludes what many scholars have called the "Lukan Gospel of the Outcast" (15:1–19:10). Its singular character lies in the fact that Luke, who devotes the whole tone of his Gospel toward embracing the poor and lowly, includes this passage,

a man there named Zacchaeus, who was a chief tax collector and also a wealthy man, ³was seeking to see who Jesus was; but he could not see him because of the crowd, for he was short in stature. ⁴So he ran ahead and climbed a sycamore tree in order to see Jesus, who was about to pass that way. ⁵When he reached the place, Jesus looked up and said to him, "Zacchaeus, come down quickly, for today I must stay at your house." ⁶And he came down quickly and received him with joy. ⁷When they all saw this, they began to grumble, saying, "He has gone to stay at the house of a sinner." ⁸But Zacchaeus stood there and said to the Lord, "Behold, half of my possessions, Lord, I shall give to the poor, and if I have extorted anything from anyone I shall repay it four times over." ⁹And Jesus said to him, "Today salvation has come to this house because this man too is a descendant of Abraham. ¹⁰For the Son of Man has come to seek and to save what was lost."

---

which focuses on the salvation of the rich and powerful. Unlike the rich official in 18:18-23, Zacchaeus does not depend on his wealth and status but on God's loving mercy to gain entry into the kingdom.

Tax collecting was a lucrative business. Romans used to sell the office to the highest bidder. For his part, the tax collector would then have to pay his contracted amount to the Romans as well as collect the fiscal revenues for them. Anything over and beyond those sums was his to keep. Failing to meet his payments would mean the Romans could confiscate his property and sell him and his family into slavery. Zacchaeus's position as the chief tax collector meant that lesser officials would have bidden for their offices from him, and if they did not produce the payment, Zacchaeus would have applied the appropriate penalties. In a word, Zacchaeus was very wealthy, and the resentment against him would have been very strong.

Despite his occupation, Zacchaeus is determined to see Jesus, even if it means looking foolish in doing so. Scholars are divided on whether to read the verbs "give" and "repay," which grammatically are in the present tense in Greek (v. 8), as present or future. In other words, is Zacchaeus boasting of present practices or making a statement of repentance to guide his future action? His hasty explanation to Jesus is heartfelt, for it would be of no advantage to him, an extortionist, to heed a wandering prophet or wonderworker. Furthermore, the fact that he does show knowledge of wrongdoing manifests the salvation that is visiting him. If Jesus comes "to seek and to save what was lost" (v.10), Zacchaeus must be a sinner. Zacchaeus the sinner can make a claim of being a descendant of Abraham, and his earnest desire to get a glimpse of Jesus is proof enough that that is what he desires.

The Parable of the Ten Gold Coins. [11]While they were listening to him speak, he proceeded to tell a parable because he was near Jerusalem and they thought that the kingdom of God would appear there immediately. [12]So he said, "A nobleman went off to a distant country to obtain the kingship for himself and then to return. [13]He called ten of his servants and gave them ten gold coins and told them, 'Engage in trade with these until I return.' [14]His fellow citizens, however, despised him and sent a delegation after him to announce, 'We do not want this man to be our king.' [15]But when he returned after obtaining the kingship, he had the servants called, to whom he had given the money, to learn what they had gained by trading. [16]The first came forward and said, 'Sir, your gold coin has earned ten additional ones.' [17]He replied, 'Well done, good servant! You have been faithful in this very small

---

19:11-27 The parable of the ten gold coins

Matthew and Luke differ in the telling of this parable, which, in large part, comes from Q overlapping slightly with Mark 13:34. A major difference between the two is that Luke also has a subtext discussing servants who do not want this particular nobleman to rule over them. This subtext may have as its origin Rome's choice of placing Archelaus, son of Herod the Great, on the throne at the death of his father. Because of his tyrannical and nearly sadistic behavior, the Jews petitioned Rome to have him removed. Rome responded by giving him only one-third of Herod's kingdom and eventually banishing him completely because of his excessive cruelty and incompetence.

Of lesser importance is Matthew's use of *talaton* (25:15) and Luke's *mna* as the denomination of the currency involved, which is translated here as "gold coins" (v. 13). A *mna* ("mina") would be worth about one hundred days' wages, and a *talanton* ("talent") sixty times as much.

Luke introduces the passage by noting that the traveling party was near Jerusalem and that some were supposing that the kingdom of God was about to appear. The parable addresses some of these points. The absentee nobleman returns without notice and thus surprises his servants. The first two servants are prepared for his sudden reappearance and are able to produce interest on the money given them; the third is not so concerned and has only a handkerchief with the original amount. It should be emphasized that the servants are commanded to use the money in such a manner as to earn more; thus the third servant was not only foolish but also disobedient.

As a story that follows the passage about the rich Zaccheus, this parable gives an example on the proper way to use riches. The metaphor

matter; take charge of ten cities.' ¹⁸Then the second came and reported, 'Your gold coin, sir, has earned five more.' ¹⁹And to this servant too he said, 'You, take charge of five cities.' ²⁰Then the other servant came and said, 'Sir, here is your gold coin; I kept it stored away in a handkerchief, ²¹for I was afraid of you, because you are a demanding person; you take up what you did not lay down and you harvest what you did not plant.' ²²He said to him, 'With your own words I shall condemn you, you wicked servant. You knew I was a demanding person, taking up what I did not lay down and harvesting what I did not plant; ²³why did you not put my money in a bank? Then on my return I would have collected it with interest.' ²⁴And to those standing by he said, 'Take the gold coin from him and give it to the servant who has ten.' ²⁵But they said to him, 'Sir, he has ten gold coins.' ²⁶'I tell you, to everyone who has, more will be given, but from the one who has not, even what he has will be taken away. ²⁷Now as for those enemies of mine who did not want me as their king, bring them here and slay them before me.'"

VI. The Teaching Ministry in Jerusalem

The Entry into Jerusalem. ²⁸After he had said this, he proceeded on his journey up to Jerusalem. ²⁹As he drew near to Bethphage and Bethany at the place called the Mount of Olives, he sent two of his disciples. ³⁰He said, "Go

---

demonstrates that goods are to be employed for the upbuilding of the kingdom, and goods that are not used for this purpose will be taken away, as we see done with the third servant's *mna*.

The Lukan subtext plays a role in this passage by representing absolute refusal on the part of some to acknowledge the kingdom of God at all, whether in Jesus' first coming or in his second. Luke concludes this subtext within the same passage by having the nobleman slay the opposition. Many often cite this passage as an example of Lukan anti-Semitism. There is nothing in it, however, to suggest that those who receive the nobleman/Christ are Gentiles or that those who do not are Jews.

With this parable Jesus' journey to Jerusalem, which begins at 9:51, has reached its destination.

THE TEACHING MINISTRY IN JERUSALEM

Luke 19:28–21:38

Jesus has taught in Galilee, along the road to Judea, and now he will teach in the holy city. He arrives in Jerusalem, the city where he will meet his passion, death, and resurrection. With this background, his teaching takes on urgency.

into the village opposite you, and as you enter it you will find a colt tethered on which no one has ever sat. Untie it and bring it here. [31]And if anyone should ask you, 'Why are you untying it?' you will answer, 'The Master has need of it.'" [32]So those who had been sent went off and found everything just as he had told them. [33]And as they were untying the colt, its owners said to them, "Why are you untying this colt?" [34]They answered, "The Master has need of it." [35]So they brought it to Jesus, threw their cloaks over the colt, and helped Jesus to mount. [36]As he rode along, the people were spreading their cloaks on the road; [37]and now as he was approaching the slope of the Mount of Olives, the whole multitude of his disciples began to praise God aloud with joy for all the mighty deeds they had seen. [38]They proclaimed:

▶

19:28-40 The entry into Jerusalem

All four Gospels contain the account of the Jesus' triumphal entry into Jerusalem. The respective narratives share a great deal of information, and any differences among them are seen in some minor details.

For all three Synoptic writers, this triumphal entry is Jesus' first and only trip to Jerusalem, but John's Gospel, along with some details among the Synoptics, shows evidence that he may have gone to Jerusalem several times during his earthly ministry. The possibility of other sojourns to Jerusalem notwithstanding, what distinguishes this visit from all the others is the reception Jesus receives.

Bethphage and Bethany are both on the Roman road from Jericho to Jerusalem. We know from John 11:17-18 that Jesus has friends at the latter. This detail would explain how he could have made arrangements for the colt beforehand (Luke 19:29-31). All four Gospels show a heavy reliance on the prophecy in Zechariah 9:9 in their depictions of the scene.

In his descent from the Mount of Olives, Jesus encounters a rejoicing crowd. Matthew and Mark mention that the crowd also set garments and branches on the way; John specifies "palm branches" (12:13) but says nothing of garments, while Luke reads "cloaks" but does not include branches (v. 36). That three of the evangelists specify branches is used as evidence by some that the scene of the entry into Jerusalem described here actually refers to an earlier one at the time of the feast of Booths, or Sukkoth, a pilgrimage celebration falling in mid-September. Either Luke's source did not include branches, or Luke saw the reference as a superfluous detail. Whether or not the entry arises from the community's memory of a fall celebration at Sukkoth or a spring feast at Passover, the pertinent detail is that Jesus arrives in Jerusalem with throngs welcoming him.

"Blessed is the king who comes
     in the name of the Lord.
Peace in heaven
     and glory in the highest."

[39] Some of the Pharisees in the crowd said to him, "Teacher, rebuke your disciples." [40] He said in reply, "I tell you, if they keep silent, the stones will cry out!"

The Lament for Jerusalem. [41] As he drew near, he saw the city and wept over it, [42] saying, "If this day you only knew what makes for peace—but now it is hidden from your eyes. [43] For the days are coming upon you when your enemies will raise a palisade against you; they will encircle you and hem you in on all sides. [44] They will smash you to the ground and your children within you, and they will not leave one stone upon another within you because you did not recognize the time of your visitation."

The other evangelists have the crowd shouting "Hosanna," an Aramaic expression meaning "Save! I pray," a phrase unfamiliar to Luke's Gentile audience. Whereas the other Gospels have *"Blessed is he* who comes in the name of the Lord," Luke reads *"Blessed is the king"* (19:38, emphasis added). Luke's phrasing links Jesus' arrival in Jerusalem to the instruction on the imminent manifestation of the kingdom of God (see 13:35; 16:16; 18:15-17).

As an echo of the angels' hymn at the birth of Jesus (Luke 2:14), the crowd shouts out, "Peace in heaven and glory in the highest" (v. 38). What angels sang at Jesus' birth people now acclaim at his arrival.

Luke's depiction of the Pharisees in the crowd is less harsh than that of Matthew, who locates them in the temple after Jesus has cleansed it (Matt 21:16). Luke situates the Pharisees along the road leading into Jerusalem, and they seem more alarmed than hostile (19:39). Jesus' answer, a hyperbolic statement of fact, also serves as a challenge (19:40).

19:41-44 The lament over Jerusalem

The first lament over the city occurs in Luke 13:34-35 and is a Q saying (see Matt 23:37-39). Here, however, the reading appears only in Luke; both in theme and in imagery it is connected to the third and final reference to Jerusalem's destruction in Luke 21:21-24. Moreover, references to the siege (v. 43) are found in Jeremiah 6:6 and Ezekiel 4:2.

From the slopes of the Mount of Olives, Jesus would have seen the whole city spread out before him on the next hill. The temple with the doors to the holy of holies would have faced him. Tradition commemorates this scene at the Church of Dominus Flevit on the Mount of Olives. Archaeological evidence indicates that the most probable gate of Jesus' entry into the city rests underneath today's Golden Gate, which has been blocked since the eighth century. Today the Palm Sunday procession en-

The Cleansing of the Temple. [45]Then Jesus entered the temple area and proceeded to drive out those who were selling things, [46]saying to them, "It is written, 'My house shall be a house of prayer, but you have made it a den of thieves.'" [47]And every day he was teaching in the temple area. The chief priests, the scribes, and the leaders of the people, meanwhile, were seeking to put him to death, [48]but they could find no way to accomplish their purpose because all the people were hanging on his words.

20 The Authority of Jesus Questioned. [1]One day as he was teaching the people in the temple area and proclaiming the good news, the chief priests and scribes, together with the elders, approached him [2]and said to

---

ters through St. Stephen's Gate, to the north of the Golden Gate along the eastern wall of the city.

19:45-48 The cleansing of the temple

Unlike Matthew or Mark, Luke concludes the entry into Jerusalem with the cleansing of the temple. Luke offers the most economic description of the event by not specifying the money changers, the animals, or even the "whip out of cords" (John 2:15). The phrase "My house shall be a house of prayer, but you have made it a den of thieves" is a blending of Isaiah 56:7 and Jeremiah 7:11.

The business transactions would have taken place in the Court of the Gentiles, surrounded by the Royal Portico, which was constructed for this very purpose. The merchants are not out of place in conducting their affairs in this area. In fact, the temple court served as the ground where worshipers proceeded from secular to sacred space by changing their pagan money to Jewish coins and purchasing ritually pure sacrificial victims. Jesus' anger, therefore, is not so much directed at those who have profaned a sacred zone with their mercantile greed; rather, he seems to be upset that any business should be associated with the temple at all. With incense, animals, oil, grain, and everything else needed for the sacrifices, the temple was a source of great income to the priests who had shares in most of the shops.

The glorious entry into Jerusalem ends on an ominous tone as the "chief priests, the scribes, and the leaders of the people" (v. 47), but not the Pharisees (19:39), plot to put Jesus to death.

20:1-8 Questioning Jesus' authority

It is natural that after such a dramatic action as cleansing the temple, the priests, scribes, and elders would question Jesus' authority. All three Synoptic Gospels feature this account within the same narrative sequence.

him, "Tell us, by what authority are you doing these things? Or who is the one who gave you this authority?" ³He said to them in reply, "I shall ask you a question. Tell me, ⁴was John's baptism of heavenly or of human origin?" ⁵They discussed this among themselves, and said, "If we say, 'Of heavenly origin,' he will say, 'Why did you not believe him?' ⁶But if we say, 'Of human origin,' then all the people will stone us, for they are convinced that John was a prophet." ⁷So they answered that they did not know from where it came. ⁸Then Jesus said to them, "Neither shall I tell you by what authority I do these things."

The Parable of the Tenant Farmers. ⁹Then he proceeded to tell the people this parable. "[A] man planted a vineyard, leased it to tenant farmers, and

---

The authority of Jesus' teaching was a major question throughout his ministry, as the earlier Beelzebul controversy substantiates (Luke 11:14-23).

The temple leaders named here comprise the Sanhedrin, the highest Jewish council. It was composed of three groups: the priests (the high priest as well as the former high priests and family representatives); the scribes (legal scholars); and the elders (the chief members of the leading families and clans). Totaling seventy-one members, this group was the official Jewish court. In Jesus' time it had jurisdiction in religious and secular affairs only in Judea, but capital cases had to be recommended to the Roman governor for approval. It met in Jerusalem within the temple complex.

Jesus' reply is structured to avoid falling into the trap the officials have fashioned. If he were to say that his authority comes from the Lord God, as indeed it does, they could accuse him of blasphemy. As it is, Jesus' response insinuates such a conclusion without providing any incriminating evidence. By referring to John the Baptist, Jesus also draws from the prophetic tradition to make his defense. The comments of the temple leaders indicate the great regard for the Baptist that many of the people held. This devotion to John has implications for the development of Christianity.

20:9-19 The wicked tenant farmers

This parable strikes a note of recognition with both the people (v. 16) and the scribes and chief priests (v. 19). The whole piece is an analogy of the prophetic tradition. The one who plants the vineyard represents God; the tenant farmers, the people; the series of servants, the various prophets; the son, Jesus. The vineyard, as a fundamental symbol of Israel, and indeed the parable itself echo Isaiah (5:1-7), but it also surfaces as such in Psalm 80. Matthew (21:39) and Luke (20:15) reflect a literal understanding of the analogy by having the tenants cast the son from the vineyard before

then went on a journey for a long time. [10]At harvest time he sent a servant to the tenant farmers to receive some of the produce of the vineyard. But they beat the servant and sent him away empty-handed. [11]So he proceeded to send another servant, but him also they beat and insulted and sent away empty-handed. [12]Then he proceeded to send a third, but this one too they wounded and threw out. [13]The owner of the vineyard said, 'What shall I do? I shall send my beloved son; maybe they will respect him.' [14]But when the tenant farmers saw him they said to one another, 'This is the heir. Let us kill him that the inheritance may become ours.' [15]So they threw him out of the vineyard and killed him. What will the owner of the vineyard do to them? [16]He will come and put those tenant farmers to death and turn over the vineyard to others." When the people heard this, they exclaimed, "Let it not be so!" [17]But he looked at them and asked, "What then does this scripture passage mean:

'The stone which the builders rejected
has become the cornerstone'?

[18]Everyone who falls on that stone will be dashed to pieces; and it will crush anyone on whom it falls." [19]The scribes and chief priests sought to lay their hands on him at that very hour, but they feared the people, for they knew that he had addressed this parable to them.

Paying Taxes to the Emperor. [20]They watched him closely and sent

killing him (see Mark 12:8). Many think that a redactor tried to align the story with Jesus' crucifixion outside the walls of Jerusalem.

The context of this passage is, of course, the altercation Jesus has with the Sanhedrin in Luke 20:1-8. They refuse to recognize the hand of God in John the Baptist, whom Herod had put to death, and they continue in their refusal to see the hand of God in Jesus. Jesus ties his claim to divine authority by quoting from Psalm 118:22-23 (Luke 20:17), a verse that also resonates with Isaiah 8:14-15.

The schism motif enters here once again (see Luke 2:34). The leaders reject Jesus, but the people do not. God's promise takes root in the vineyard Israel, represented by the people's response, but this vineyard will also be shared with the Gentiles (v. 16).

Luke uses the parable's imagery and interpretation in Acts (18:6; 28:28). It also resurfaces in other New Testament writings, such as Romans 11:17-18 and 1 Peter 2:6-7.

20:20-26 Paying taxes to Caesar

The scribes and the chief priests are relentless in their attempts to trap Jesus by catching him off guard. After being shamed by the parable of the

agents pretending to be righteous who were to trap him in speech, in order to hand him over to the authority and power of the governor. ²¹They posed this question to him, "Teacher, we know that what you say and teach is correct, and you show no partiality, but teach the way of God in accordance with the truth. ²²Is it lawful for us to pay tribute to Caesar or not?" ²³Recognizing their craftiness he said to them, ²⁴"Show me a denarius; whose image and name does it bear?" They replied, "Caesar's." ²⁵So he said to them, "Then repay to Caesar what belongs to Caesar and to God what belongs to God." ²⁶They were unable to trap him by something he might say before the people, and so amazed were they at his reply that they fell silent.

tenant farmers (20:9-19), they now send spies or agents to Jesus with hopes that he might incriminate himself by speaking against the empire. Jesus, however, sees through the ruse (20:23).

Roman coinage was highly symbolic for Jews concerned about paying taxes to the emperor. Engraved on the face of the denarius was the image of Tiberius Caesar—at the very least an offense against Jewish sensibilities, since it would go against the prohibition of graven idols. As a subject people, the Jews were required to use this currency for paying taxes and tribute to their occupiers. The question about the legality of paying taxes, therefore, involves the legality of handling idols to do so; the religious Jew should not be in contact with such pagan objects. Combined with these religious principles was the humiliation of paying the conqueror in the coin that transgressed their law code, thus forcing the Jews to participate in Roman paganism. Jesus' response not only avoids the trap the leaders set for him but also calls into question the meaning of true, righteous behavior.

Jesus gains the upper hand against his adversaries by not pitting allegiance to Rome against fidelity to the Torah (the holy writings of the Jewish religion, especially the first five books of the Old Testament). The lesson is that one is not defiled by paying taxes to Rome. Being righteous before God is an issue deeper than paying taxes to a pagan power.

The idea of rendering to Caesar the things that are Caesar's and to God the things that are God's has often been mistakenly used as an injunction for keeping religious and ethical questions separate from political or secular policies. Correctly read through an eschatological lens, Jesus' aphorism states that the things of this world have an impact on the next, while standards of the age to come should have an influence on this present life.

The Question about the Resurrection. ²⁷Some Sadducees, those who deny that there is a resurrection, came forward and put this question to him, ²⁸saying, "Teacher, Moses wrote for us, 'If someone's brother dies leaving a wife but no child, his brother must take the wife and raise up descendants for his brother.' ²⁹Now there were seven brothers; the first married a woman but died childless. ³⁰Then the second ³¹and the third married her, and likewise all the seven died childless. ³²Finally the woman also died. ³³Now at the resurrection whose wife will that woman be? For all seven had been married to her." ³⁴Jesus said to them, "The children of this age marry and remarry; ³⁵but those who are deemed worthy to attain to the coming age and to the resurrection of the dead neither marry nor are given in marriage. ³⁶They can no longer die, for they are like angels; and they are the children of God because they are the ones who will rise. ³⁷That the dead will rise even Moses made known in the passage about the bush, when he called 'Lord' the God of Abraham, the God of Isaac, and the God of Jacob; ³⁸and he is not God of the dead, but of the living,

---

20:27-40 Sadducees and the resurrection

The Sadducees, opponents of the Pharisees, particularly over the teachings on the resurrection, are the next group to question Jesus with an eye toward tripping him up. Not much is known about them except that they were aristocratic conservatives tied to the temple cult (unlike the Pharisees, who promoted the synagogue movement). The circumstance they describe is based on levirate marriage (Deut 25:5-6), whereby a widow's brother-in-law marries her to ensure that the lands stay in the first husband's family and that his name is carried on. Jesus responds by discussing first the nature of a resurrected life and then the basis of the resurrection in the Jewish tradition.

The resurrected life goes beyond the dimensions of earthly existence. Thus expectations and practices in this world do not hold in the next. Moreover, the resurrected life transcends this one (vv. 35, 36, 38). By citing Moses, Jesus taps the source of Jewish faith as well as the sole component of the Sadducees' teaching, for their belief extended no further than the first five books of Moses, often called the Torah or the Pentateuch.

Jesus' argument is impeccable. The scribes, who along with the Pharisees believe in the resurrection, affirm Jesus' answer; the Sadducees who brought up the matter, on the other hand, are silent (vv. 39-40).

Unlike the parallel accounts in Matthew 22:23-33 or Mark 12:18-27, Luke's version contains a teaching that supports celibate life (v. 35; see also Matt 19:12)

for to him all are alive." ³⁹Some of the scribes said in reply, "Teacher, you have answered well." ⁴⁰And they no longer dared to ask him anything.

The Question about David's Son. ⁴¹Then he said to them, "How do they claim that the Messiah is the Son of David? ⁴²For David himself in the Book of Psalms says:

'The Lord said to my lord,
"Sit at my right hand
⁴³till I make your enemies your
footstool."'

⁴⁴Now if David calls him 'lord,' how can he be his son?"

Denunciation of the Scribes. ⁴⁵Then, within the hearing of all the people, he said to [his] disciples, ⁴⁶"Be on guard against the scribes, who like to go around in long robes and love greetings in marketplaces, seats of honor in synagogues, and places of honor at banquets. ⁴⁷They devour the houses of widows and, as a pretext, recite lengthy prayers. They will receive a very severe condemnation."

20:41-44 David's Son

Jesus' opponents would want to make sure that there is nothing about him which would suggest that he is the Messiah. At the same time, they have to acknowledge that the people see him as a great man, and therefore he could quite possibly be the one long promised by the prophets. At that time the tradition existed of a Messiah arising from David's line, a belief to which the infancy narratives attest. The narrative here draws on this tradition.

In verse 42 Jesus cites Psalm 110:1, a coronation psalm, which in the Greek Septuagint is reflected in this translation. In Psalm 110 the psalmist is speaking, and "Lord" (uppercase here) refers to Yahweh. The "lord" (lowercase here) is the king whom Yahweh is placing on the throne. In its New Testament interpretation, "Lord" still refers to Yahweh, but David the king is speaking. Consequently, "lord" represents a messianic figure who is greater than David. In these verses Jesus states that the term "lord" refers to himself.

The early church drew on this tradition of a Davidic Messiah both here and elsewhere, and this psalm was used as one of the Old Testament writings prefiguring Christ. The other Synoptics contain passages parallel to this one.

20:45-47 Denunciation of the scribes

Jesus, after defending himself before both the Pharisees and Sadducees, takes the offensive. Scribes, as ones who could read, write, and interpret texts, are synonymous with the Pharisees. As a scholarly religious class who knew the Torah and the oral tradition with all the astuteness of master lawyers, they expected honor and deference as their due. As with

21 The Poor Widow's Contribution.

¹When he looked up he saw some wealthy people putting their offerings into the treasury ²and he noticed a poor widow putting in two small coins. ³He said, "I tell you truly, this poor widow put in more than all the rest; ⁴for those others have all made offerings from their surplus wealth, but she, from her poverty, has offered her whole livelihood."

The Destruction of the Temple Foretold.

⁵While some people were speaking about how the temple was adorned with costly stones and votive offerings, he said, ⁶"All that you see here—the days will come when there will not be left a stone upon

all professions, there were good and bad members among them. Even Jesus was considered by his disciples to be a teacher.

The condemnation Jesus levels here (vv. 46-47) is directed toward those who are a part of the temple power structure and use their status and expertise for personal advantage at the expense of the poor and underprivileged. This short passage also reflects the debates between church and synagogue in the early days of the Christian movement. It sets the context for what follows in Luke 21:1-4.

21:1-4 The poor widow's contribution

Luke shares this story with Mark (see Mark 12:41-44). Each coin is a *lepton*, which is worth slightly more than one-hundredth of a denarius. Since a denarius is a day's wage, the widow places about one-fiftieth of a day's living into the treasury, and, as Jesus remarks, this is her whole livelihood.

Many hold that this story shows the widow's pious devotion, and she has become a model of religious dedication in that all should give from their sustenance and not their superfluity. The context, however, suggests another interpretation.

Jesus' first order of business upon entering Jerusalem is to go to the temple and drive out those "selling things" (19:45). His violent response to revenues generated by temple worship in that section of the Lukan narrative would be indicative of anger here. In addition, in the preceding passage Jesus has denounced the scribes for "devour[ing] the houses of widows" (Luke 20:47). Jesus is upset at seeing a poor woman think that God's will demanded making herself destitute so that others could become rich.

21:5-6 The destruction of the temple foretold

All three Synoptics contain the prediction of the temple's destruction. The building of Herod's temple, the edifice under discussion in this

another stone that will not be thrown down."

The Signs of the End. ⁷Then they asked him, "Teacher, when will this happen? And what sign will there be when all these things are about to happen?" ⁸He answered, "See that you not be deceived, for many will come in my name, saying, 'I am he,' and 'The time has come.' Do not follow them! ⁹When you hear of wars and insurrections, do not be terrified; for such things must happen first, but it will not immediately be the end." ¹⁰Then he said to them, "Nation will rise against nation, and kingdom against kingdom. ¹¹There will be powerful earthquakes, famines, and plagues from place to place; and awesome sights and mighty signs will come from the sky.

passage, began in 19 B.C. and was still under construction during Jesus' lifetime (see John 2:20). The whole complex was completed in A.D. 64, only to be totally razed six years later during the First Jewish Revolt. When it was completed, it was considered one of the most beautiful buildings in the whole Roman Empire. The people's awe and wonder at the stones were totally justified. As the house of God, its destruction would seem like the end of the world in the minds of the people (see Josephus, *Ant.* 15.11.1-7 and *J.W.* 4-5).

Is the prediction of the destruction a *vaticinium ex eventu,* that is, a foretelling after the event? If so, then the writer, Luke, is theologizing about the temple's destruction by placing a prediction of it on the lips of Jesus. On the other hand, anyone sensitive to the political climate of the day would know that the tensions would someday explode, resulting in catastrophic disaster for the nation.

This account forms a bridge between the story of the poor widow (21:1-4) and Luke's apocalyptic section (21:7-36).

21:7-11 The signs of the end

Luke 21:7-36 forms the Lukan apocalypse, but it is not the only place in the Third Gospel where apocalyptic imagery occurs (see Luke 17:22-37). Matthew 24 and Mark 13 have parallel passages.

The great part of the language and metaphor used here is characteristic of apocalyptic writing: signs, natural upheavals, disasters, wars, persecution, and a call to vigilance. Apocalyptic language is often, but not exclusively, associated with eschatological teaching, and in this sense this section is more rightly called the Lukan eschatological discourse. By definition, *eschatology* deals with the interpretation of the end times, the fulfillment of history, and culmination of human destiny. In

The Coming Persecution. [12]"Before all this happens, however, they will seize and persecute you, they will hand you over to the synagogues and to prisons, and they will have you led before kings and governors because of my name. [13]It will lead to your giving testimony. [14]Remember, you are not to prepare your defense beforehand, [15]for I myself shall give you a wisdom in speaking that all your adversaries will be powerless to resist or refute. [16]You will even be handed over by parents, brothers, relatives, and friends, and they will put some of you to death. [17]You will be hated by all because of my name, [18]but not a hair on your head will be destroyed. [19]By your perseverance you will secure your lives.

The Great Tribulation. [20]"When you see Jerusalem surrounded by armies, know that its desolation is at hand. [21]Then those in Judea must flee to the mountains. Let those within the city escape from it, and let those in the countryside not enter the city, [22]for these days are the time of punishment when all the scriptures are fulfilled. [23]Woe to pregnant women and nursing

---

general, we can say that this section shows eschatological concerns in apocalyptic language.

Rarely has anyone been able to identify conclusively the particular historical references to the events mentioned in verses 7-11. There has never been a time in human history when wars, earthquakes, famines, and plagues have not been a part of the picture. Since any one of these events and phenomena can occur without warning or notice, it is better to be prepared, and preparation consists in always looking for Christ in every person and circumstance.

21:12-19 The coming persecution

The early Christian community faced persecution from the home as well as from rulers of both synagogue and state. These Gospel verses, in non-apocalyptic vocabulary, are meant to console and strengthen the believers facing their tribulation.

Verses 14-15 form a doublet with Luke 12:11-12.

21:20-24 The great tribulation

The words that Jesus speaks in this passage ring true to the history of the destruction of Jerusalem.

The Roman general Titus arrived at Jerusalem and set up his main camp about one mile north of the Mount of Olives at Mount Scopus in the spring of A.D. 70. By July his men set to constructing a siege wall around the city to prevent the people of Jerusalem from escaping while protecting the Roman soldiers from Jewish raiding parties. Since such procedures

mothers in those days, for a terrible calamity will come upon the earth and a wrathful judgment upon this people. ²⁴They will fall by the edge of the sword and be taken as captives to all the Gentiles; and Jerusalem will be trampled underfoot by the Gentiles until the times of the Gentiles are fulfilled.

The Coming of the Son of Man. ²⁵"There will be signs in the sun, the moon, and the stars, and on earth nations will be in dismay, perplexed by the roaring of the sea and the waves. ²⁶People will die of fright in anticipa-tion of what is coming upon the world, for the powers of the heavens will be shaken. ²⁷And then they will see the Son of Man coming in a cloud with power and great glory. ²⁸But when these signs begin to happen, stand erect and raise your heads because your re-demption is at hand."

The Lesson of the Fig Tree. ²⁹He taught them a lesson. "Consider the fig tree and all the other trees. ³⁰When their buds burst open, you see for yourselves and know that summer is now near; ³¹in the same way, when you see these

---

were standard Roman military operations, the description in these verses need not be considered peculiar to the Roman siege in A.D. 70. Nonethe-less, the arrival of the Romans came with unexpected suddenness, and in-ternecine fighting among various Jewish sects had reduced the food stores, so that starvation became a major problem within the city (see Jose-phus, *J.W.* 5.2-3i). On August 28 (Ninth of Ab, by coincidence the same day the Babylonians breached the city some six hundred years earlier), Je-rusalem fell to the Romans. Any Jewish survivors were taken captive, and the city, including the temple, was razed to the ground.

Old Testament prophecies are employed in the description: Hosea 9:7 in Luke 21:22; Sirach 28:18; Deuteronomy 28:64; and Zechariah 12:3 in Luke 21:24. Tradition has it that the Christians in the city fled to the city of Pella in present-day Jordan at the outbreak of hostilities. The "time of the Gentiles" (v. 24) foreshadows the great missionary ventures outlined in the Acts of the Apostles.

21:25-28 The coming of the Son of Man

The scene shifts from Jerusalem to the whole world. The language re-turns to apocalyptic terminology, drawing on Isaiah, Joel, Zephaniah, and Daniel. What has happened to Jerusalem may be a harbinger of the Son of Man's visitation upon the earth, but it is not an immediate warning signal. The scene is not bleak, however. The astral signs and natural calamities serve to notify that redemption is at hand. Just as the people of Jerusalem were mixed in their reception of Jesus, so too will the world be at his sec-ond coming.

things happening, know that the kingdom of God is near. ³²Amen, I say to you, this generation will not pass away until all these things have taken place. ³³Heaven and earth will pass away, but my words will not pass away.

Exhortation to be Vigilant. ³⁴"Beware that your hearts do not become drowsy from carousing and drunkenness and the anxieties of daily life, and that day catch you by surprise ³⁵like a trap. For that day will assault everyone who lives on the face of the earth. ³⁶Be vigilant at all times and pray that you have the strength to escape the tribulations that are imminent and to stand before the Son of Man."

Ministry in Jerusalem. ³⁷During the day, Jesus was teaching in the temple area, but at night he would leave and stay at the place called the Mount of Olives. ³⁸And all the people would get up early each morning to listen to him in the temple area.

21:29-33 The lesson of the fig tree

If people can read the signs in nature, they should be willing and able to read the signs of their deliverance.

The reference to "this generation" (v. 32) is ambiguous. In one sense, there is every reason to believe that many in the then contemporary generation would not pass away until after the First Jewish Revolt. On the other hand, if "all these things" refers to upheavals in nature ushering in the Son of Man, "this generation" is a timeless reference to the world; the *eschaton*, or end time, is always imminent.

21:34-36 Exhortation to be vigilant

One must stand with apocalyptic vigilance. The note of surprise resurfaces here (v. 34). Under an imminent understanding of the *eschaton*, the coming of the Son of Man will always be sudden. The directive to pray (v. 36) is a particularly Lukan concern. Jesus prays in the Garden of Gethsemane (22:39-46), and his note of "tribulations" (v. 36) looks toward his own passion.

21:37-38 Conclusion to the ministry in Jerusalem

During the pilgrimage feasts most people, particularly those without relatives in Jerusalem proper, camped on the fields and hills surrounding the city. The Mount of Olives appears to have been one such place.

Despite the discourse on the temple and Jerusalem, Luke is ambiguous toward both. Jesus teaches in the temple even as he speaks against it. Furthermore, in the Acts of the Apostles the temple becomes the site of many events in the ministry of Peter, Paul, and the other disciples. Jesus' public ministry ends with these verses.

VII. The Passion Narrative

22 **The Conspiracy against Jesus.** [1]Now the feast of Unleavened Bread, called the Passover, was drawing near, [2]and the chief priests and the scribes were seeking a way to put him to death, for they were afraid of the people. [3]Then Satan entered into Judas, the one surnamed Iscariot, who was counted among the Twelve, [4]and he went to the chief priests and temple guards to discuss a plan for handing him over to them. [5]They were pleased and agreed to pay him money. [6]He accepted their offer and sought a favorable opportunity to hand him over to them in the absence of a crowd.

Preparations for the Passover. [7]When the day of the feast of Unleavened Bread arrived, the day for sacrificing the Passover lamb, [8]he sent out Peter and John, instructing them, "Go

---

THE PASSION

Luke 22:1–23:56

The passion narrative, the nucleus of the kerygma, forms the oldest part of the Gospel tradition. The accounts of the four evangelists show the greatest similarity with each other in this section. Nonetheless, each evangelist shapes the information to fit the theological architecture of his respective Gospel. In Luke, the themes found all along reach their climax. The schism motif, the great reversal, and the victory over evil all manifest Jesus' reclamation of the cosmos from Satan's clutches as Christ brings the promise of future glory to all.

22:1-6 The conspiracy against Jesus

The diabolical force that has been mounting challenge against Jesus from the very beginning (Luke 4:1-13) increases in intensity here when Satan "enter[s] into Judas" (v. 3). In Luke's narrative, now is the "time" (4:13) for which the devil has been waiting.

Both priests and scribes are at the center of the conspiracy, but by making Judas his agent, Satan fashions a more serious inroad against Jesus. Hence the passion is not merely a human drama; rather, it is an event that involves the whole cosmos. Luke's account of Jesus' passion, with its collusion between Satan and Judas, departs from the synoptic presentation and aligns itself more closely with the Johannine text, and in so doing respects the cosmological nature of the drama.

One of the major pilgrimage feasts that brought thousands to Jerusalem, the feast of Unleavened Bread was originally an agrarian festival celebrated in the spring during the grain harvest. Passover began as a nomadic feast, also held in the spring, when people took their flocks of

and make preparations for us to eat the Passover." ⁹They asked him, "Where do you want us to make the preparations?" ¹⁰And he answered them, "When you go into the city, a man will meet you carrying a jar of water. Follow him into the house that he enters ¹¹and say to the master of the house, 'The teacher says to you, "Where is the guest room where I may eat the Passover with my disciples?"' ¹²He will show you a large upper room that is furnished. Make the preparations there." ¹³Then they went off and found everything exactly as he had told them, and there they prepared the Passover.

The Last Supper. ¹⁴When the hour came, he took his place at table with the apostles. ¹⁵He said to them, "I have eagerly desired to eat this Passover with you before I suffer, ¹⁶for, I tell you, I shall not eat it [again] until there is fulfillment in the kingdom of God." ¹⁷Then he took a cup, gave thanks, and said, "Take this and share it among yourselves; ¹⁸for I tell you [that] from this time on I shall not drink of the fruit of the vine until the kingdom of God comes." ¹⁹Then he took the bread, said the blessing, broke it, and gave it to them, saying, "This is my body, which will be given for you; do this in memory

---

sheep and goats from the winter to summer feeding grounds. The Jewish practice at the time of Jesus had joined these two feasts into one commemorating the Exodus from Egypt.

For the Romans, this annual spring holiday posed a major security risk. The throngs of people, coupled with the nationalistic overtones inherent in the Exodus event, set the stage for riots and insurrection. The temple leaders, functioning as colonial lackeys of Rome, were well aware that Jesus was a popular figure who fulfilled the messianic expectations of a great many. A conspiracy between Judas, the chief priests, and the guards that tries to find an opportunity to arrest Jesus away from the crowd is indicative of the volatility of the situation (v. 6).

22:7-38 The Passover meal

According to the synoptic dating, the meal takes place on Passover (v. 7); in John's Gospel (13:1) it is on the day before. Jesus must have had disciples and acquaintances in Jerusalem for him to give such specific instructions to Peter and John (vv. 10-12). For this reason, many scholars believe that Jesus went to Jerusalem on several occasions and not just this once, as Luke and the other Synoptics portray. Since women alone generally carried water jars, a man walking with one would attract attention. Jesus leaves the exact location for the meal unspecified to maintain secrecy in the face of impending danger. The Greek for "guest room" (v. 11) is *kataluma* (see 2:7).

of me." ²⁰And likewise the cup after they had eaten, saying, "This cup is the new covenant in my blood, which will be shed for you.

The Betrayal Foretold. ²¹"And yet behold, the hand of the one who is to betray me is with me on the table; ²²for the Son of Man indeed goes as it has been determined; but woe to that man by whom he is betrayed." ²³And they began to debate among themselves who among them would do such a deed.

The Role of the Disciples. ²⁴Then an argument broke out among them about which of them should be regarded as the greatest. ²⁵He said to them, "The kings of the Gentiles lord it over them and those in authority over them are addressed as 'Benefactors'; ²⁶but among you it shall not be so. Rather, let the greatest among you be as the youngest, and the leader as the servant. ²⁷For who is greater: the one seated at table or the one who serves? Is it not the one seated at table? I am among you as the one who serves. ²⁸It is you who have stood by me in my trials; ²⁹and I confer a kingdom on you, just as my Father has conferred one on me, ³⁰that you may eat and drink at my table in my kingdom; and you will sit on thrones judging the twelve tribes of Israel.

Peter's Denial Foretold. ³¹"Simon, Simon, behold Satan has demanded to sift all of you like wheat, ³²but I have prayed that your own faith may not

---

It is nearly impossible to determine with absolute accuracy the Jewish Seder, that is, the Passover meal, at this period of history. Nonetheless, all indications are that it involved a total of three blessings of the cup. Luke mentions two of them—one at the beginning of the meal and one at the end (vv. 17, 20). Paul's version of what has come to be called the "institution narrative" is remarkably similar to that of Luke here (see 1 Cor 11:23-26). The elements of the Exodus sacrifice, such as blood, are reinterpreted in the light of Christ's life. He sheds his blood to ensure the life of God's people (see Exod 12:12-16; 24:5-8).

The mention of the betrayer's hand (v. 21), whom the reader knows to be Judas Iscariot (22:3), sparks an argument at the table. Jesus intervenes with a lesson that continues the reversal theme introduced in the *Magnificat* (Luke 1:46-55). Here at the Last Supper, Jesus gives a more positive rendition of the theme: disciples should reverse the roles themselves in order to further the kingdom. Doing so leads to true greatness (22:24-30).

Just as Jesus predicts the role of Judas, though unnamed (vv. 21-23), so too does he predict Peter's denial (vv. 31-34). The devil has already claimed Judas, and now he is attempting to take the rest of the Twelve, Peter included, as Jesus is well aware. Jesus needs Peter to support the others (v. 32), but Peter will falter, as Jesus predicts. Luke alone acknowledges in this manner the cosmic battle Jesus' life and death entail.

fail; and once you have turned back, you must strengthen your brothers." ³³He said to him, "Lord, I am prepared to go to prison and to die with you." ³⁴But he replied, "I tell you, Peter, before the cock crows this day, you will deny three times that you know me."

Instructions for the Time of Crisis. ³⁵He said to them, "When I sent you forth without a money bag or a sack or sandals, were you in need of anything?" "No, nothing," they replied. ³⁶He said to them, "But now one who has a money bag should take it, and likewise a sack, and one who does not have a sword should sell his cloak and buy one. ³⁷For I tell you that this scripture must be fulfilled in me, namely, 'He was counted among the wicked';

and indeed what is written about me is coming to fulfillment." ³⁸Then they said, "Lord, look, there are two swords here." But he replied, "It is enough!"

The Agony in the Garden. ³⁹Then going out he went, as was his custom, to the Mount of Olives, and the disciples followed him. ⁴⁰When he arrived at the place he said to them, "Pray that you may not undergo the test." ⁴¹After withdrawing about a stone's throw from them and kneeling, he prayed, ⁴²saying, "Father, if you are willing, take this cup away from me; still, not my will but yours be done." ⁴³[And to strengthen him an angel from heaven appeared to him. ⁴⁴He was in such agony and he prayed so fervently that his sweat became like drops of blood

---

In a crisis one should be sure to prepare for the worst, a worry not present in easier times (vv. 35-37). The Twelve still have difficulty understanding Jesus' teaching and mission. They take his metaphors literally, and he loses patience (v. 38).

22:39-53 The agony and arrest

Jesus goes to the Mount of Olives, as is his custom (21:37-38). Prayer is a key element in the makeup of Luke's Gospel, and at this moment Jesus prays. The disciples, however, oblivious to the seriousness of events, fall asleep.

Many reliable ancient manuscripts do not include verses 43-44, but many other ones, just as reliable, do. Whether these verses belong in the Lukan text is a debated issue, but the balance tips for their inclusion. In Luke's temptation scene (4:1-13), the devil "depart[s] for a time," and because he does, Luke has no need of including the ministering angels found in Matthew 4:11 and Mark 1:13. In Luke's narrative, Satan's time comes at the passion (22:3, 31). With Luke, therefore, the angel comes to minister to Jesus during his agony, the time and place where Satan exhibits his fury; it is Satan's "hour, the time for the power of darkness" (v. 53), an "hour" that will last through the crucifixion (see 23:44).

falling on the ground.] ⁴⁵When he rose from prayer and returned to his disciples, he found them sleeping from grief. ⁴⁶He said to them, "Why are you sleeping? Get up and pray that you may not undergo the test."

The Betrayal and Arrest of Jesus. ⁴⁷While he was still speaking, a crowd approached and in front was one of the Twelve, a man named Judas. He went up to Jesus to kiss him. ⁴⁸Jesus said to him, "Judas, are you betraying the Son of Man with a kiss?" ⁴⁹His disciples realized what was about to happen, and they asked, "Lord, shall we strike with a sword?" ⁵⁰And one of them struck the high priest's servant and cut off his right ear. ⁵¹But Jesus said in reply, "Stop, no more of this!" Then he touched the servant's ear and healed him. ⁵²And Jesus said to the chief priests and temple guards and elders who had come for him, "Have you come out as against a robber, with swords and clubs? ⁵³Day after day I was with you in the temple area, and you did not seize me; but this is your hour, the time for the power of darkness."

Peter's Denial of Jesus. ⁵⁴After arresting him they led him away and took him into the house of the high priest; Peter was following at a distance. ⁵⁵They lit a fire in the middle of the courtyard and sat around it, and Peter sat down with them. ⁵⁶When a maid saw him seated in the light, she

---

Jesus' emotional state is fragile, and he prays. The road from Jerusalem to the Judean desert passes up and over the Mount of Olives. He agonizes over a decision on whether to stay or to flee, and the tension brings him to the verge of a nervous breakdown (v. 44). A rare medical condition called "hematidrosis," a bloody sweat, sometimes occurs in people under extreme duress. For this reason some speculate that Jesus actually sweat blood. The text reads, however, that his "sweat became like drops of blood," that is, heavy and thick.

Judas finds his opportunity to hand Jesus over as he had planned with the temple authorities. It is unclear from Luke whether he actually kisses Jesus, although Matthew and Mark say so. Luke, the evangelist of "sweet mercy," is the only Synoptic to have Jesus heal the ear of the high priest's slave, while John's is the only Gospel to state the slave's name (John 18:10). Jesus' followers are ready to fight, but Jesus forbids them (v. 51).

22:54-65 Peter's denial

Peter's denial is recounted in all four Gospels.

Peter, always impetuous, follows as Jesus is led to the house of the high priest. Presumably the other disciples are hiding or at least keeping their distance from Jerusalemites. Fear overpowers Peter's usually forward manner, and he denies any contact or involvement with Jesus. Luke

143

looked intently at him and said, "This man too was with him." [57]But he denied it saying, "Woman, I do not know him." [58]A short while later someone else saw him and said, "You too are one of them"; but Peter answered, "My friend, I am not." [59]About an hour later, still another insisted, "Assuredly, this man too was with him, for he also is a Galilean." [60]But Peter said, "My friend, I do not know what you are talking about." Just as he was saying this, the cock crowed, [61]and the Lord turned and looked at Peter; and Peter remembered the word of the Lord, how he had said to him, "Before the cock crows today, you will deny me three times." [62]He went out and began to weep bitterly. [63]The men who held Jesus in custody were ridiculing and beating him. [64]They blindfolded him and questioned him, saying, "Prophesy! Who is it that struck you?" [65]And they reviled him in saying many other things against him.

Jesus before the Sanhedrin. [66]When day came the council of elders of the people met, both chief priests and scribes, and they brought him before their Sanhedrin. [67]They said, "If you are the Messiah, tell us," but he replied to them, "If I tell you, you will not believe,

mentions that Jesus looks at Peter once the crowing has stopped. The glance acts as an acknowledgement of the action; Peter cannot hide from Jesus or himself, so he goes off weeping bitterly. His denial, followed by his remorse, displays Satan's near capture of him as well as the power of Jesus' prayer, for Peter, unlike Judas, will return (22:32).

Jesus spends the night in the house of the high priest, located, according to tradition and some scholars, on the southwestern slope of the city at a site currently called St. Peter in Gallicantu. Other archaeologists place the high priest's house on top of the western hill. Luke mentions only the priests and temple guards as ridiculing and demeaning Jesus here (vv. 64-65); the Romans will have their turn (23:36-37).

22:66-71 Jesus before the Sanhedrin

The Sanhedrin heard all cases dealing with Jewish law but could not inflict capital punishment, the penalty for blasphemy. Thus Jesus also has to undergo proceedings in a Roman court. The Sanhedrin uses this opportunity, therefore, to build their case before presenting him to Pilate, where they supplement the charge against Jesus with treasonable offenses (23:2).

The interrogation scene echoes details from the annunciation of Jesus' birth (1:32, 35). Jesus responds to the questions by quoting from Daniel 7:13, a text that asserts the divinity of the Messiah and thereby places the Sanhedrin under Jesus' judgment. They recognize his ploy immediately and hasten him to Pontius Pilate.

⁶⁸and if I question, you will not respond. ⁶⁹But from this time on the Son of Man will be seated at the right hand of the power of God." ⁷⁰They all asked, "Are you then the Son of God?" He replied to them, "You say that I am." ⁷¹Then they said, "What further need have we for testimony? We have heard it from his own mouth."

23 **Jesus before Pilate.** ¹Then the whole assembly of them arose and brought him before Pilate. ²They brought charges against him, saying, "We found this man misleading our people; he opposes the payment of taxes to Caesar and maintains that he is the Messiah, a king." ³Pilate asked him, "Are you the king of the Jews?" He said to him in reply, "You say so." ⁴Pilate then addressed the chief priests and the crowds, "I find this man not guilty." ⁵But they were adamant and said, "He

---

23:1-5 Jesus before Pilate

Like every colonial power in history, the Romans made friends with a certain class of the native population. This enabled them to impose foreign rule by wearing a domestic mask. In Palestine the temple priests were the class whom the Romans supported and who supported the Romans. They received revenues from performing the sacrifices of the people. In addition, they had shares in many of the shops and food providers of Jerusalem, and during the great pilgrimage feasts like Passover, this provided them with a healthy income. Roman stability secured the priests' status.

The Romans, on the other hand, needed the priests to guarantee their legitimacy. The priests enabled the Romans to appear as supporters of the Jewish faith. They acted as mediators between the emperor and the Jewish people, and as such they made Roman tax collection easier. In sum, there was an elite ruling class composed of Romans and Jews, both of whom had a vested interest in keeping the peace and suppressing any insurrection. Jesus, whose very presence garners crowds and who often questions the abuse by the authorities, presents a major threat to both parties.

Pontius Pilate's official residence was in the cosmopolitan seaport of Caesarea Maritima, Herod the Great's magnificent construction project. Within the amphitheater at the northern end was found a stone tablet incised with Pilate's name. From the Gospel accounts and Josephus, we know that Pilate went to Jerusalem only to strengthen the Roman presence among the crowds of pilgrims visiting the city during the Passover feast.

Pontius Pilate was not the weak, misinformed, and vacillating leader many think he was, and Luke notes his barbarity (13:1). The emphasis in this passage on Jesus' innocence is Luke's way of stressing that Jesus was

is inciting the people with his teaching throughout all Judea, from Galilee where he began even to here."

Jesus before Herod. [6]On hearing this Pilate asked if the man was a Galilean; [7]and upon learning that he was under Herod's jurisdiction, he sent him to Herod who was in Jerusalem at that time. [8]Herod was very glad to see Jesus; he had been wanting to see him for a long time, for he had heard about him and had been hoping to see him perform some sign. [9]He questioned him at length, but he gave him no answer. [10]The chief priests and scribes, meanwhile, stood by accusing him harshly. [11][Even] Herod and his soldiers treated him contemptuously and mocked him, and after clothing him in resplendent garb, he sent him back to Pilate. [12]Herod and Pilate became friends that very day, even though they had been enemies formerly. [13]Pilate then summoned the chief priests, the rulers, and the people [14]and said to them, "You brought this man to me and accused him of inciting the people to revolt. I have conducted my investigation in your presence and have not found this man guilty of the charges you have brought against him, [15]nor did Herod, for he sent him back to us. So no capital crime has been committed by him. [16]Therefore I shall have him flogged and then release him." [17]

---

not crucified for being a common insurrectionist (although that is the accusation), as many early Christian detractors at that time were saying.

In all of ancient literature, the only extant record of a Roman criminal court proceeding is the New Testament account of Jesus' trial before Pilate. Despite the variations of the trial among the four evangelists, their narrative lines are all quite similar: questioning by Pilate along with hesitancy on his part over Jesus' guilt; release of a criminal named Barabbas in Jesus' place; and a handing over of Jesus for crucifixion.

23:6-12 Jesus before Herod

Luke alone features this account. Herod Antipas, the son of Herod the Great, is the Jewish client-king of Galilee and Perea, and he is probably in Jerusalem for the Passover feast. Because Jesus is originally from Galilee, Pilate sends him to Herod as a diplomatic courtesy. The two leaders had been at enmity with each other, probably because of Pilate's slaughter of Galileans (13:1), but Pilate's action here reconciles the two.

Herod has an interest in Jesus (9:9), and it appears that he wishes to see some spectacle (23:8). Jesus never indulges in such displays. Consequently, Herod and his soldiers mock Jesus, as the Roman soldiers will do in 23:36. Jesus is returned to Pilate, where he is condemned. The Christian tradition sees this episode as a prophetic fulfillment of Psalm 2:1-2. See Acts 4:25-28.

The Sentence of Death. [18]But all together they shouted out, "Away with this man! Release Barabbas to us." [19](Now Barabbas had been imprisoned for a rebellion that had taken place in the city and for murder.) [20]Again Pilate addressed them, still wishing to release Jesus, [21]but they continued their shouting, "Crucify him! Crucify him!" [22]Pilate addressed them a third time, "What evil has this man done? I found him guilty of no capital crime. Therefore I shall have him flogged and then release him." [23]With loud shouts, however, they persisted in calling for his crucifixion, and their voices prevailed. [24]The verdict of Pilate was that their demand should be granted. [25]So he released the man who had been imprisoned for rebellion and murder, for whom they asked, and he handed Jesus over to them to deal with as they wished.

The Way of the Cross. [26]As they led him away they took hold of a certain Simon, a Cyrenian, who was coming in from the country; and after laying the cross on him, they made him carry it behind Jesus. [27]A large crowd of people followed Jesus, including many women who mourned and lamented him. [28]Jesus turned to them and said, "Daughters of Jerusalem, do not weep for me; weep instead for yourselves and for your children, [29]for indeed, the

23:13-25 The sentence of death

The Gospel presentation of a vacillating Pilate is most apparent in this scene. Any information about releasing a prisoner in honor of the holiday we have from Matthew, Mark, and John, but not Luke (ancient and dependable manuscripts omit v. 17, which appears to have been an added gloss prompted by the readings in Matthew 27:15 and Mark 15:6). Luke simply mentions that Pilate releases Barabbas (v. 25). The Gospels are the only source we have that mentions this custom; ancient Roman historians never refer to such a policy. Is Luke, or the other evangelists for that matter, relating a historical fact? Scholars are divided on the issue. In any case, the guilty Barabbas serves as a point of comparison with the innocent Jesus.

23:26-32 The way of the cross

Crucifixion was a feared form of execution that the Romans reserved for slaves, subject populations, and the lowest criminals. The vertical shaft of the cross usually remained standing at the place of execution for successive use and to serve as a grim warning to the resident population. To add to their shame, the condemned were stripped naked and made to carry their own crossbeam amidst the jeers, taunts, and jabs of the crowd.

The Romans press Simon the Cyrenian into service, not because they pitied Jesus, but because they wanted to ensure that he lived long enough to undergo the ignominious death. By following behind Jesus, Simon be-

days are coming when people will say, 'Blessed are the barren, the wombs that never bore and the breasts that never nursed.' ³⁰At that time people will say to the mountains, 'Fall upon us!' and to the hills, 'Cover us!' ³¹for if these things are done when the wood is green what will happen when it is dry?" ³²Now two others, both criminals, were led away with him to be executed.

The Crucifixion. ³³When they came to the place called the Skull, they crucified him and the criminals there, one on his right, the other on his left. ³⁴[Then Jesus said, "Father, forgive them, they know not what they do."] They divided his garments by casting lots. ³⁵The people stood by and watched; the rulers, meanwhile, sneered at him and said, "He saved others, let him save himself if he is the chosen one, the Messiah of God." ³⁶Even the soldiers jeered at him. As they approached to offer him wine ³⁷they called out, "If you are King of the Jews, save yourself." ³⁸Above him there

comes a model disciple, a point that would be important for the Cyrenians who formed part of the early Christian community (Acts 11:20; 13:1). The Gnostics, who denied the humanity of Jesus, will claim that Jesus was swept into heaven at the crucifixion and that Simon was mistakenly nailed to the cross, an interpretation that early Christian writers effectively counter.

People are following Jesus on the way (v. 27), and Luke's schism motif again surfaces; some are disciples, others are not. Luke often shows people divided along lines of discipleship, and this episode provides an example of that theme. The words to the "daughters of Jerusalem" (vv. 28-30), who bear a strong resemblance to a Greek chorus, reflect the scene described in the Lukan apocalyptic material (21:6-28). Here the context is one of forgiveness.

23:33-43 The crucifixion

Luke does not use the term "Golgatha"; he simply calls the area of crucifixion the "place called the Skull" (v. 33), which at the time of Christ was located outside the walls of Jerusalem. The spot of both the crucifixion and burial have been venerated as such since the second century, and the Basilica of the Holy Sepulchre has covered the place since the time of Empress Helena. The biblical, historical, and archaeological records confirm the area marked by the basilica as the true spot of Jesus' death, burial, and resurrection.

In this section there is another bracketed verse: "Father, forgive them, they know not what they do" (23:34), probably one of the most gentle verses in the whole Bible. Nearly the same manuscripts that do not include

149

was an inscription that read, "This is the King of the Jews."

^{39}Now one of the criminals hanging there reviled Jesus, saying, "Are you not the Messiah? Save yourself and us." ^{40}The other, however, rebuking him, said in reply, "Have you no fear of God, for you are subject to the same condemnation? ^{41}And indeed, we have been condemned justly, for the sentence we received corresponds to our crimes, but this man has done nothing criminal." ^{42}Then he said, "Jesus, remember me when you come into your kingdom." ^{43}He replied to him, "Amen, I say to you, today you will be with me in Paradise."

The Death of Jesus. ^{44}It was now about noon and darkness came over the whole land until three in the after-

---

22:43-44 are the ones that also exclude this one. Although scholars are also divided on whether this verse should be part of the original text, a strong case can be made for its inclusion. In addition to its presence in dependable manuscripts, the verse certainly fits with the theme of forgiveness that runs through Luke's whole Gospel, including the passion (22:49-51).

While Luke has Herod's men alone ridiculing Jesus in 23:11, the evangelist situates the mocking by the Roman soldiers here at verses 36-37. Matthew and Mark mention that the two criminals revile Jesus, but only Luke provides a dialogue in which one criminal reprimands the other. At this point Jesus again utters words of mercy, and again we see the schism motif, with one criminal acknowledging Jesus and the other cursing him.

Throughout the crucifixion and death, there are intentional echoes from Psalm 22, Isaiah 53, Wisdom 2–3. These Old Testament works become the lens through which the kerygma is interpreted.

23:44-49 The death of Jesus

Luke's portrayal of the death of Jesus has important differences from the other two Synoptics. As the scene opens, we read of the description of the three hours of darkness. Luke adds the detail about the eclipse of the sun (v. 45). An eclipse is impossible during a full moon, which would have been the case during Passover. This verse should be read, therefore, as a circumstantial phrase well translated as "while the sun's light failed." If there is any historical background to three hours of darkness, it is most likely attributable to a dust storm coming from the desert, which is a common occurrence in this area during the spring of the year. The important point, however, is to see this passage as an echo of the many apocalyptic prophecies and writings that describe the Day of the Lord as one in which the sun will not shine (see Isa 13:10; Amos 8:9).

noon ⁴⁵because of an eclipse of the sun. Then the veil of the temple was torn down the middle. ⁴⁶Jesus cried out in a loud voice, "Father, into your hands I commend my spirit"; and when he had said this he breathed his last. ⁴⁷The centurion who witnessed what had happened glorified God and said, "This man was innocent beyond doubt." ⁴⁸When all the people who had gathered for this spectacle saw what had happened, they returned home beating their breasts; ⁴⁹but all his acquaintances stood at a distance, including the women who had followed him from Galilee and saw these events.

The tearing of the temple veil in Luke comes before the death of Jesus and not after it, as it does in Matthew and Mark. Luke is a fine literary artist, and by such a placement of the verse, he constructs the ripping of the curtain as a part of the buildup to the death of Jesus, the climax of the passage. The tearing of the veil itself is laden with a great deal of Old Testament symbolism. We really have no way of knowing to which of the several veils in the temple Luke (or the other evangelists) is referring. The bigger question is whether Luke sees the tearing as a means to let the divine presence out or the means to allow humans in. Since this Lukan version occurs before the death of Jesus, letting the divine presence out is the better conclusion. This is the day of the Lord, and God's presence, his judgment, now centers on the cross.

Among the four Gospels, there are three versions of Jesus' last words from the cross. In each case Christ's final utterance is an expression of each evangelist's theology, which for Luke is trust in God. Jesus shows absolute confidence in the Father during this last moment, a mood quite different from his prayer on the Mount of Olives (22:39-46). With the word "Father," Luke connects this last prayer with the two other prayers Jesus has spoken throughout his passion: the agony (22:42) and the prayer for forgiveness (23:34). See also the prayer for the disciples (10:21) and the Lord's Prayer (11:2).

The centurion offers the first reaction and therefore the first interpretation of Jesus' death in verse 47. The statement that Jesus is innocent (or righteous, just) recalls the deliberations of the Sanhedrin, Pilate, and Herod. On another level, the use of "innocent/righteous/just" harks back to the passage from Wisdom 3:1-3: "But the souls of the just are in the hand of God, / and no torment shall touch them. / They seemed, in the view of the foolish, to be dead; / and their passing away was thought an affliction / and their going forth from us, utter destruction. / But they are in peace." Luke sees the centurion's statement as an act of glorification of

The Burial of Jesus. ⁵⁰Now there was a virtuous and righteous man named Joseph who, though he was a member of the council, ⁵¹had not consented to their plan of action. He came from the Jewish town of Arimathea and was awaiting the kingdom of God. ⁵²He went to Pilate and asked for the body of Jesus. ⁵³After he had taken the body down, he wrapped it in a linen cloth and laid him in a rock-hewn tomb in which no one had yet been buried. ⁵⁴It was the day of preparation, and the sabbath was about to begin. ⁵⁵The women who had come from Galilee with him followed behind, and when they had seen the tomb and the way in which his body was laid in it, ⁵⁶they returned and prepared spices and perfumed oils. Then they rested on the sabbath according to the commandment.

God. Jesus has accomplished his "exodus," which he set out to do in 9:31. The "hour . . . of darkness" (22:53) has passed; it is now the hour of the Lord's glorification, ushered in by Jesus' loud cry from the cross (v. 46), a paraphrase of Psalm 31:6.

In the last two verses of the death scene, Luke portrays another dichotomy among several people; he separates the disciples and acquaintances from onlookers and mockers. The emphasis on the eyewitnesses will become an important point for the early church and will be used against those Gnostic detractors who would deny Jesus' actual death by crucifixion.

The Lukan proclivity to emphasize God's mercy becomes evident with the breast-beating onlookers as they return to their homes. The only other occurrence in Luke of breast-beating is in the parable of the Pharisee and the tax collector (18:9-14). In that parable the tax collector knows his sinfulness and asks for forgiveness. The onlookers, like the tax collector, know their sinfulness and depart asking for forgiveness. From Jesus' prayer from the cross, "Father, forgive them, they know not what they do" (23:34), we know that forgiveness is already there.

In Christian piety, verses 34, 43, and 46 are counted among the seven last words of Christ (see also Matt 27:46/Mark 15:34; John 19:26, 28, 30).

23:50-56 The burial of Jesus

The inclusion of the detail "a rock-hewn tomb in which no one had yet been buried," mentioned in some fashion in all four Gospels, underscores that Jesus' body is not laid in a tomb as part of a multiple burial. The evangelists stress that the tomb is new and unused. This detail later becomes important for the early church in countering Gnostic and Jewish charges that Jesus' body was confused among the corpses. All the activity has to be completed before the sabbath begins at sundown.

VIII. The Resurrection Narrative

24 The Resurrection of Jesus.
[1]But at daybreak on the first day of the week they took the spices they had prepared and went to the tomb. [2]They found the stone rolled away from the tomb; [3]but when they entered, they did not find the body of the Lord Jesus. [4]While they were puzzling over this, behold, two men in

---

Joseph of Arimathea, like Simeon and Anna in the infancy narrative (2:25-38), awaits the "kingdom of God" (v. 51). With him, Jesus' universal message penetrates the Sanhedrin and, ironically, has a positive effect there. Joseph's concern for extending the legal prescriptions regarding burial of the dead ensures that Jesus is not totally excommunicated from his own nation. The women disciples from Galilee (8:1-3) are faithful throughout Jesus' ministry, are present at the crucifixion, and for the burial (v. 56).

THE RESURRECTION

Luke 24:1-53

Discrepancies among the four Gospel accounts reflect the oral transmission of the stories. Each Gospel account relates the respective evangelist's theological interpretation of the fact that Jesus bodily rose on the first day of the week.

Resurrection accounts among the four Gospels can be arranged in several categories. First, there are those dealing with the empty tomb on the first day of the week. Second, there are Jesus' appearances in Jerusalem and environs. And third, there are his appearances in Galilee. All four Gospels feature accounts of the empty tomb, and, to a greater or lesser extent, they all recount appearances in Jerusalem. Luke's is the only one, however, that does not contain any narratives of the Galilean appearances. On the other hand, the most protracted Jerusalem story (24:13-35) is found only in the Third Gospel. Because the second volume to the Lukan corpus, the Acts of the Apostles, relates the whole missionary venture of the church as starting in Jerusalem and from there "throughout Judea and Samaria, to the ends of the earth" (Acts 1:8), Christ's presence in Galilee is simply folded into the broader picture with references to the spice-bearing women (23:55-56) and the "men of Galilee" (Acts 1:11).

24:1-12 The resurrection of Jesus

Tombs were often sealed with a large, wheel-like stone that was rolled in a carved trench in front of a rectangular doorway. Several strong men

dazzling garments appeared to them. [5]They were terrified and bowed their faces to the ground. They said to them, "Why do you seek the living one among the dead? [6]He is not here, but he has been raised. Remember what he said to you while he was still in Galilee, [7]that the Son of Man must be handed over to sinners and be crucified, and rise on the third day." [8]And they remembered his words. [9]Then they returned from the tomb and announced all these things to the eleven and to all the others. [10]The women were Mary Magdalene, Joanna, and Mary the mother of James; the others who accompanied them also told this to the apostles, [11]but their story seemed like nonsense and they did not believe them. [12]But Peter got up and ran to the tomb, bent down, and saw the burial cloths alone; then he went home amazed at what had happened.

The Appearance on the Road to Emmaus. [13]Now that very day two of them were going to a village seven miles from Jerusalem called Emmaus, [14]and they were conversing about all the things that had occurred. [15]And it happened that while they were conversing and debating, Jesus himself drew near and walked with them, [16]but their eyes were prevented from recognizing him. [17]He asked them, "What are you dis-

were needed to move it. The lowly status of women in ancient society not only kept them from politics, but it also meant that they were not to be taken seriously. Paradoxically, this condition gave them some power, since they could come and go in the most volatile areas without raising suspicion, as their standing at the crucifixion and their visit to the tomb attest. Mary Magdalene is the only woman witness common to all four Gospels. For this reason, she has been called *apostola apostolorum,* the "apostle of the apostles."

That the stone has been rolled away when the women arrive is the first sign of something out of the ordinary. Luke has men, described in angel-like terms, stilling the women's fear and placing the resurrection in the context of Jesus' teaching and ministry. The men do not command the women to tell the others, but the women do so out of their own joy and enthusiasm, a truly Lukan ideal of the faithful disciple, and these women have not yet seen the risen Lord. Unfortunately, the men remain incredulous of the women's story, although Peter finds it sufficiently convincing to see for himself.

24:13-35 The road to Emmaus

The spice-bearing women have spread the word concerning the empty tomb, so the disciples in town know about it (24:9). One of the disciples along the road is called Cleopas (v. 18), a name similar to Klopas, the hus-

cussing as you walk along?" They stopped, looking downcast. [18]One of them, named Cleopas, said to him in reply, "Are you the only visitor to Jerusalem who does not know of the things that have taken place there in these days?" [19]And he replied to them, "What sort of things?" They said to him, "The things that happened to Jesus the Nazarene, who was a prophet mighty in deed and word before God and all the people, [20]how our chief priests and rulers both handed him over to a sentence of death and crucified him. [21]But we were hoping that he would be the one to redeem Israel; and besides all this, it is now the third day since this took place. [22]Some women from our group, however, have astounded us: they were at the tomb early in the morning [23]and did not find his body; they came back and reported that they had indeed seen a vision of angels who announced that he was alive. [24]Then some of those with us went to the tomb and found things just as the women had described, but him they did not see." [25]And he said to them, "Oh, how foolish you are! How slow of heart to believe all that the prophets spoke! [26]Was it not necessary that the Messiah should suffer these things and enter into his glory?" [27]Then beginning with Moses and all the prophets, he interpreted to them what referred to him in all the scriptures. [28]As they approached the village to which they were going, he gave the impression that he was going on farther. [29]But they urged him, "Stay with us, for it is nearly evening and the day is almost over." So

band of one of the women at the cross, according to John's Gospel (19:25). Many have speculated with good reason that the two mentioned here are married to each other.

Luke is the only Gospel to present this passage, and there may be historical accuracy associated with it. At least three towns lay claim to being the Emmaus of this pericope. The text says that it is situated sixty stadia from Jerusalem, which is the distance for the round trip between the city and Emmaus, a walk one could make at that hour of the day, especially if as excited and enthusiastic as these two disciples. The Emmaus matching most of the criteria lies opposite present-day Moza, whose ruins from the 1948 war are still visible.

The reply to Jesus' questions summarizes the ministry as disciples would have seen and understood it (vv. 17-24). Jesus' explanation places all the events within the context of Old Testament prophecies and Jewish experience (vv. 25-27). They recognize him in the breaking of the bread, a detail reiterated when they relate the story to the Eleven and the others. They can fully *see* who Jesus is, however, and therefore *believe* in him only once the "traveling companion" explains the Law and the prophets. None of this information is new to these disciples; they are merely hearing it

he went in to stay with them. ³⁰And it happened that, while he was with them at table, he took bread, said the blessing, broke it, and gave it to them. ³¹With that their eyes were opened and they recognized him, but he vanished from their sight. ³²Then they said to each other, "Were not our hearts burning [within us] while he spoke to us on the way and opened the scriptures to us?" ³³So they set out at once and returned to Jerusalem where they found gathered together the eleven and those with them ³⁴who were saying, "The Lord has truly been raised and has appeared to Simon!" ³⁵Then the two recounted what had taken place on the way and how he was made known to them in the breaking of the bread.

The Appearance to the Disciples in Jerusalem. ³⁶While they were still speaking about this, he stood in their midst and said to them, "Peace be with you." ³⁷But they were startled and terrified and thought that they were seeing a ghost. ³⁸Then he said to them, "Why are you troubled? And why do questions arise in your hearts? ³⁹Look at my hands and my feet, that it is I myself. Touch me and see, because a ghost does not have flesh and bones as you can see I have." ⁴⁰And as he said this, he showed them his hands and his feet. ⁴¹While they were still incredulous for

again as though for the first time, and the little hope they may have had has blossomed into faith: "Were not our hearts burning [within us] while he spoke to us on the way and opened the scriptures to us?" (v. 32). This passage presents a balance between the word (vv. 25-27) and sacrament (vv. 30-32), and as such, it is highly eucharistic and liturgical. See also Mark 16:12-13.

By specifically using "eleven" (v. 33) instead of "apostles," Luke highlights Judas's betrayal and prepares the narrative for the election of his replacement in Acts 1:15-26.

24:36-49 The appearance in Jerusalem

Maintaining that the resurrected Jesus is a ghost is more comprehensible to the disciples than believing that he is risen. With this Jerusalem appearance, paralleled in John 19:19-29, Luke presents an apology for those who deny the reality of the resurrection. He does so by having Jesus call the question on the nature of his current existence (v. 39a). Jesus then allows the disciples to feel his flesh and bone while he presents the marks of the crucifixion (vv. 39b-40). Finally, he expresses hunger, and they give him fish to eat. Because it symbolizes overabundance, fish is a sign of the eschatological age, which Jesus' resurrection has indeed ushered in.

As he does with the disciples on the road to Emmaus, Jesus here explains his life, ministry, and resurrection in light of the Old Testament

joy and were amazed, he asked them, "Have you anything here to eat?" ⁴²They gave him a piece of baked fish; ⁴³he took it and ate it in front of them.

⁴⁴He said to them, "These are my words that I spoke to you while I was still with you, that everything written about me in the law of Moses and in the prophets and psalms must be fulfilled." ⁴⁵Then he opened their minds to understand the scriptures. ⁴⁶And he said to them, "Thus it is written that the Messiah would suffer and rise from the dead on the third day ⁴⁷and that repentance, for the forgiveness of sins, would be preached in his name to all the nations, beginning from Jerusalem. ⁴⁸You are witnesses of these things. ⁴⁹And [behold] I am sending the promise of my Father upon you; but stay in the city until you are clothed with power from on high."

The Ascension. ⁵⁰Then he led them [out] as far as Bethany, raised his

---

prophecies and experience. The role of the disciples as witnesses to these events is emphasized. They are to start in Jerusalem before heading to the nations. This geographical plan is restated in Acts 1:8. The "power from on high" (v. 49) is the Holy Spirit, who descends upon them in Jerusalem (Acts 2:1-13).

This passage introduces the nature of the glorified body, a reality that goes to the heart of Christian belief. The resurrected life that Christ initiates goes beyond spiritual existence in eternity. It is a new life involving the glorified body that is not immediately recognizable to friends and loved ones, and therefore different from the mortal body, yet this glorified body has continuity with the mortal one. The glorified body transcends the limits of time and space, and yet it is physical. Wounds and blemishes are apparent, yet they do not scar or cause pain. Not much more can be said on the nature of the resurrected body than what Luke describes here. Luke wants faithful believers to know that the same destiny awaits them (see Acts 2:14-41).

24:50-53 The ascension

Luke recapitulates the ascension in the Acts of the Apostles (1:6-12), with some additions. The two ascension stories serve as a bridge connecting the two-volume work. Here it occurs on the same day as the resurrection; in Acts, it begins the apostolic ministry. This ascension account completes the journey to Jerusalem (9:51), while it also ends the Gospel. Jesus' exodus, first voiced in 9:31, is completed with the glorious ascension.

The road to Bethany passes over the Mount of Olives. Jesus was last on the mount during his agony and arrest, when the hour of the "power of darkness" held sway (22:53). His presence on the Mount of Olives now is the triumph over the dark power of Satan.

hands, and blessed them. [51]As he blessed them he parted from them and was taken up to heaven. [52]They did him homage and then returned to Jerusalem with great joy, [53]and they were continually in the temple praising God.

In Scripture, the Mount of Olives is considered the hill of God's judgment and glorification, and it takes on that role here. Jesus raises his hands in the Old Testament priestly blessing, he ascends gloriously into heaven, and the disciples are filled with joy. Although the Spirit does not come until they are gathered together at Pentecost (Acts 2:1-4), they participate even now in Christ's glorification by praising God in the temple (v. 53). They are the models for all Christians who await the fullness of Christ's reign.

REVIEW AIDS AND DISCUSSION TOPICS

Introduction *(pages 5–7)*

1. What was the central reason each evangelist wrote his Gospel?

2. What does Luke's Gospel tell us about him?

3. How does Luke view the passion, death, and resurrection of Jesus?

4. Luke relies on four literary motifs to relay his key concepts. If you were writing a gospel, what would be your key concepts and how would you present them to your readers?

1:1-4 Prologue *(pages 9–10)*

1. Luke was writing for an audience of converts—Gentiles living in a pagan world. How would you introduce your gospel to your audience today?

1:5–2:52 The Infancy Narrative *(pages 10–22)*

1. Luke's account of the birth of Christ centers on Mary, while Matthew's centers on Joseph. Compare the two accounts and evaluate this statement.

2. What are some of the prophecies and typologies (things that are prefigured or symbolized by things in the Old Testament) Luke uses in the Infancy Narrative? How do they help your understanding of the message of Luke's Gospel?

3. How does Luke show in the Infancy Narrative that Jesus is the fulfillment of both the Jewish and Gentile cultural worlds?

4. What is Luke's theological purpose in including the historical information in his section on the birth of Jesus?

5. Which of the four literary motifs does Luke use in his Infancy Narrative? Do you think they are effective in conveying the "good news" of Jesus' entry into salvation history? Why?

3:1–4:13 The Preparation for the Public Ministry *(pages 23–29)*

1. Why do you think Luke begins this section with historical detail, as he did in the birth of Jesus?

2. What is John the Baptist's role in the story of Jesus? What was the purpose of John's baptism?

3. What role does the Holy Spirit play in the preparation of Jesus for his ministry?

4. Why does Luke take Jesus' family tree all the way back to Adam while Matthew begins only with Abraham? Do you know anything about the people named as Jesus' ancestors?

5. What are Jesus' three temptations? Why does their order in Luke differ from Matthew's? How might these temptations apply to your life?

4:14–9:50 The Ministry in Galilee *(pages 29–69)*

1. How does Luke continue the schism motif in this section?

2. How does faith manifest itself in the four stories in chapter 5? How would their meeting Jesus affect the future lives of these people?

3. In view of the global community and globalization, how might Luke's Sermon on the Plain (6:20-49) apply to the people of today, both in and outside the church? Take one part of the Sermon and think about it in light of this question.

4. Give modern examples of the kinds of response to the word of God indicated in the explanation of the parable of the sower (8:11-15).

5. Give examples of Luke's use of his great reversal motif in 9:1-50. Can you think of times in your life when you have glimpsed, or clearly seen, that indeed the messianic age has arrived and the kingdom of God is here, now?

9:51–19:27 The Journey to Jerusalem *(pages 69–125)*

1. Why is Jesus so severe with those seeking to accompany him to Jerusalem (9:51-62)? At what point in your own life did you make an adult decision to follow Jesus on his way?

2. Compare the stories of the Good Samaritan and Martha and Mary (10:25-42) as instructions on Christian discipleship. When have you found yourself called to be a Good Samaritan?

3. During his journey to Jerusalem, what does Jesus say about the cost of discipleship? What does he say about vigilance on the part of disciples? Have you ever experienced the cost of discipleship?

4. Which structures in our society support trust in God and which support trust in possessions (14:13-34; 16:1-15)?

5. Why does heaven rejoice more over the one repentant sinner than over the ninety-nine righteous (15:1-10)? What is the difference between "righteous" and "self-righteous"?

6. Luke 15:1–19:10 has been called the "Lukan Gospel of the Outcast." What kinds of outcasts does Luke write about and what does Jesus do for them? Who are some of the outcasts in our society? Have you ever felt like or found yourself an outcast and did your experience help you empathize with society's outcasts?

19:28–21:38 The Teaching Ministry in Jerusalem *(pages 125–138)*

1. How does Jesus defend his authority as God's appointed teacher when he is confronted in the temple (chapter 20)?

2. What did Jesus mean by his response to the question about taxes (20:20-25)? Is it ever wrong to pay taxes? Why?

3. What signs of the "end times" do you think are present in our day? As those who follow the teaching of Jesus, what do you think our response should be?

22:1–23:56 The Passion *(pages 139–153)*

1. According to Luke, the passion is an event which involves the whole cosmos. How does Luke show this?

2. According to Luke, the passion is Satan's "hour, the time for the power of darkness." Among the people who appear in chapters 22 and 23, who succumb to the darkness and who do not? Have you ever experienced the power of darkness? How did you overcome it?

3. When is the power of darkness defeated and all creation redeemed?

24:1-53 The Resurrection *(pages 153–158)*

1. The two Emmaus disciples recognize Jesus "in the breaking of the bread." Do you think this shows that there were disciples, besides the Twelve, at the Last Supper? In light of Luke's treatment of women

throughout his Gospel, do you think it likely that there were women at the Last Supper?

2. All through his Gospel, Luke has shown how Jerusalem is central to the mission of the infant church. How does he underscore that fact in chapter 24?

3. If we are to consider ourselves disciples of Christ, then we must carry on the mission of the church, to bring salvation to all people. How do you think you take part in this mission?

INDEX OF CITATIONS FROM THE
CATECHISM OF THE CATHOLIC CHURCH

The arabic number(s) following the citation refers to the paragraph number(s) in the *Catechism of the Catholic Church.* The asterisk following a paragraph number indicates that the citation has been paraphrased.

Luke

Citation	Paragraph	Citation	Paragraph	Citation	Paragraph
1:11	332*	1:54-55	706*	3:21	608,* 2600*
1:15-19	724*	1:55	422*	3:22	536*
1:15	717	1:68	422,* 717	3:23	535*
1:17	523, 696, 716,* 718, 2684*	1:73	706*	4:1	695*
1:23	1070*	1:76	523	4:5-6	2855*
1:26-38	497,* 706,* 723,* 2571*	2:6-7	525*	4:8	2096*
1:26-27	488	2:7	515*	4:9	2119*
1:26	332*	2:8-20	486,* 525*	4:13	538
1:28-37	494*	2:8-14	333*	4:16-22	1286*
1:28	490, 491	2:10	333	4:16-21	436*
1:31	430,* 2812*	2:11	437, 448,* 695*	4:18-19	695,*714
1:32-33	709*	2:14	333, 559,* 725*	4:18	544, 2443*
1:32	559	2:19	2599*	4:19	1168*
1:34	484, 497,*505	2:21	527*	5:8	208
1:35	437, 484, 486,* 697	2:22-39	529,* 583*	5:16	2602*
1:37-38	494	2:25	711*	5:17	1116*
1:37	148, 269,* 273, 276	2:26–27	695*	5:30	588*
1:38	64,* 148, 510, 2617,* 2677, 2827,* 2856,*	2:32	713*	5:32	588
		2:34	575, 587*	6:6-9	581*
		2:35	149,* 618*	6:12-16	1577*
1:41	523,* 717, 2676	2:38	711*	6:12	2600*
1:43	448,* 495, 2677	2:41-52	534*	6:19	695,* 1116,* 1504
1:45	148, 2676	2:41	583*	6:20-22	2444*
1:46-55	722,* 2619,* 2675*	2:46-49	583*	6:20	2546*
		2:48-49	503*	6:24	2547
1:46-49	2097*	2:49	2599	6:28	1669*
1:48	148,* 971, 2676,*	2:51-52	531	6:31	1789,* 1970*
1:49	273, 2599,* 2807,* 2827*	2:51	517,* 2196, 2599*	6:36	1458*, 2842
		2:52	472	7:11-17	994*
1:50	2465*	3:3	535*	7:16	1503
		3:8	1460	7:18-23	547*
		3:10-14	535	7:19	453*
		3:11	2447	7:22	544*
		3:16	696	7:26	523,* 719
				7:36-50	2712*

7:36	575,* 588*	11:20	700	16:22	336,* 1021*
7:37-38	2616*	11:21-22	385*	17:1	2287
7:48	1441	11:37	588	17:3-4	2845*
8:6	2731*	11:39-54	579*	17:4	2227*
8:10	1151*	11:41	2447	17:5	162*
8:13-15	2847*	12:1-3	678*	17:14	586*
8:13	2731*	12:6-7	342	17:19-31	2463*
8:15	368,* 2668*	12:8-9	333*	17:33	1889
8:24	2743*	12:10	1864*	18:1-8	2573,* 2613*
8:26-39	550*	12:12	1287*	18:1	2098
8:46	695,* 1116*	12:13	549*	18:8	675*
9:2	551	12:14	549*	18:9-14	2559,* 2613*
9:18-20	2600*	12:32	764	18:9	588
9:23	1435*	12:35-40	2849*	18:13	2631, 2667,*
9:28	2600*	12:49	696		2839*
9:30-35	2583*	12:50	536,* 607,*	19:1-10	2712*
9:31	554, 1151*		1225,* 2804*	19:8	549,* 2412
9:33	556*	13:15-16	582*	19:9	1443*
9:34-35	659,* 697	13:20-21	2660*	19:11-27	1936*
9:35	516, 554	13:31	575*	19:13	1880*
9:45	554*	13:33	557	19:15	1880*
9:51	557	13:35	585*	19:38	559*
9:58	544*	14:1	575,* 588*	19:41-42	558
10:1-2	765*	14:3-4	582*	20:17-18	587*
10:2	2611*	14:26	1618*	20:36	330*
10:7	2122*	14:33	2544	20:39	575*
10:16	87, 858*	15	1443,* 1846*	21:4	2544*
10:17-20	787*	15:1-2	589*	21:12	675*
10:21-23	2603*	15:7	545	21:24	58,* 674*
10:21	1083*	15:11-32	545,* 2839*	21:27	671,* 697*
10:25-37	2822*	15:11-31	1700*	21:34-36	2612*
10:27-37	1825*	15:11-24	1439	22:7-20	1151,* 1339
10:27	2083*	15:18	1423,* 2795*	22:14	2804*
10:34	1293*	15:21	2795*	22:15-16	1130
11:1	520,* 2601,	15:23-32	589*	22:15	607*
	2759, 2773	15:32	1468	22:18	1403*
11:2-4	2759*	16:1	952*	22:19-20	1365
11:2	2632*	16:3	952*	22:19	610, 611,*621,
11:4	1425, 2845	16:13	2424		1328, 1381
11:5-13	2613*	16:16	523*	22:20	612*
11:9	2761	16:18	2382*	22:26-27	894*
11:13	443,* 728,*	16:19-31	1859,* 2831*	22:27	1570*
	2623,*2671*	16:22-26	633*	22:28-30	787*

22:29-30	551*	23:46	730,* 1011,*	24:31	659*
22:30	765*		2045	24:34	552,* 641
22:31-32	641,* 643*	23:47	441*	24:36	641, 645*
22:32	162,* 552,*	24:1	641,* 2174	24:38	644*
	2600*	24:3	640*	24:39	644,* 645,* 999
22:40	2612*	24:5-6	626, 640	24:40	645*
22:41-44	2600*	24:6-7	652*	24:41-43	645*
22:42	532, 2605,	24:9-10	641	24:41	644
	2824	24:11	643	24:43	2605
22:43	333*	24:12	640*	24:44-48	652*
22:46	2612*	24:13-49	1094*	24:44-46	112*
22:61	1429	24:13-35	1329,* 1347*	24:44-45	572, 601*
22:70	443	24:15	645,* 659*	24:44	702,* 2625,*
23:2	596*	24:17	643		2763*
23:19	596	24:21	439*	24:45	108
23:28	2635*	24:22-23	640*	24:46	627
23:34	591,* 597,*	24:25-27	112,* 601*	24:47-48	730*
	2605, 2635*	24:26-27	572, 652*	24:47	981, 1120,*
23:39-43	440,* 2616*	24:26	555, 710*		1122
23:40-43	2266*	24:27	555,* 2625*	24:48-49	1304*
23:43	1021*	24:30	645*, 1166*	24:51	659*

Palestine in the Time of Jesus

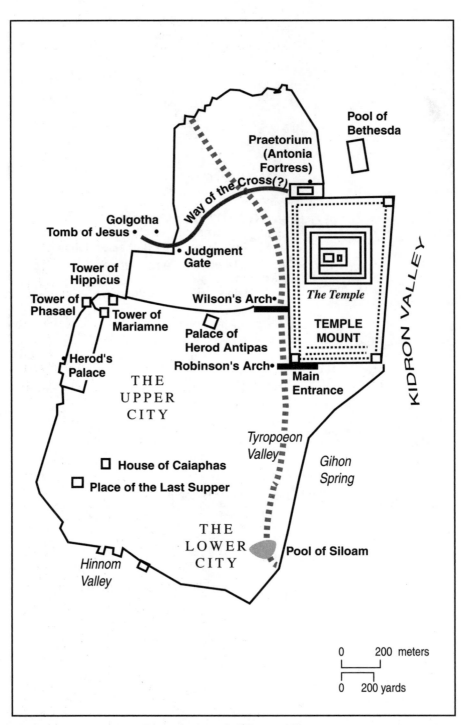

Pool of
Bethesda

Praetorium
(Antonia
Fortress)

Way of the Cross(?)

Golgotha
Tomb of Jesus • •

Judgment
Gate

Tower of
Hippicus

Tower of
Phasael

Tower of
Mariamne

Palace of
Herod Antipas

Wilson's Arch•

The Temple

TEMPLE
MOUNT

Robinson's Arch•

Main
Entrance

Herod's
Palace

THE
UPPER
CITY

☐ House of Caiaphas

☐ Place of the Last Supper

*Tyropoeon
Valley*

*Gihon
Spring*

THE
LOWER
CITY

Pool of Siloam

*Hinnom
Valley*

KIDRON VALLEY

0   200 meters

0   200 yards

Jerusalem in the Time of Jesus